Ensuring Every Child Matters

Gianna Knowles

Los Angeles | London | New Delhi
Singapore | Washington DC

First published 2009

Reprinted 2009

SAGE Publications Ltd
1 Oliver's Yard
55 City Road
London EC1Y 1SP

SAGE Publications Inc.
2455 Teller Road
Thousand Oaks, California 91320

SAGE Publications India Pvt Ltd
B 1/I 1 Mohan Cooperative Industrial Area
Mathura Road
New Delhi 110 044

SAGE Publications Asia-Pacific Pte Ltd
33 Pekin Street #02–01
Far East Square
Singapore 048763

Library of Congress Control Number: 2008937154

British Library Cataloguing in Publication data

A catalogue record for this book is available from the
British Library

ISBN 978–1-84860–136-9
ISBN 978–1-84860–137-6 (pbk)

Typeset by Dorwyn, Wells, Somerset
Printed in Great Britain by CPI Antony Rowe,
Chippenham, Wiltshire
Printed on paper from sustainable resources

Mixed Sources
Product group from well-managed
forests and other controlled sources
www.fsc.org Cert no. SGS-COC-2953
FSC © 1996 Forest Stewardship Council

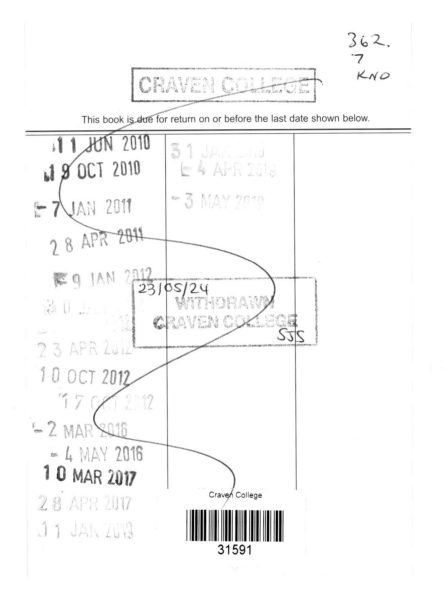

Contents

For Jeremy, Matthew and Rebecca

Acknowledgements

A number of the case studies used in this book have been contributed by friends and colleagues. In particular I would like to thank Ann Parker, Children's Centre Manager, Kent; Vanessa Smith, Foundation Degree in Teaching and Learning Support, University of Chichester; Katherine Wardlaw, Foundation Degree in Teaching and Learning Support, University of Chichester and Jamie Atkins, BA Primary Education and Teaching, University of Chichester.

About the Author

Gianna Knowles is a Senior Lecturer in Education at the University of Chichester. She has over 12 years' experience of working in primary schools in London and across the country. She has worked in the education advisory service, working with individual teachers and whole-school staffs to develop practice and policies in these areas. She has experience of being an OfSTED Inspector and reviewer for the Quality and Assurance Agency (QAA). Gianna's research interest is in the area of social justice and inclusion.

Key for icons

Chapter objectives

Activities

Case studies

Further reading

Useful websites

Introduction

The Children Act 2004 heralded a significant change in the way services that are directly concerned with serving children and families need to organize, manage and offer their provision. As a result of consultation with children and families, following Lord Laming's enquiry into the terrible and tragic death of Victoria Climbié, the government announced its plans for how children's services would be restructured to help achieve five outcomes for well-being. The government outlined these outcomes in its Every Child Matters (ECM) agenda, stating that to achieve well-being in childhood and in later life children and young people want to:

- be healthy;
- be safe;
- enjoy and achieve;
- make a positive contribution; and
- achieve economic well-being (DfES, 2004b).

These five outcomes for well-being are now the goals for the Every Child Matters agenda and all services that are concerned for the education and welfare of children and young people are bound to ensure these outcomes are achieved.

One of the further aspects of the change to children's services that has happened as a result of the Every Child Matters agenda is the restructuring of children's services, including education, child protection, health and the Youth Criminal Justice system to ensure all these services are working together to provide a multi-agency approach to enabling the five outcomes to be met. Therefore, each agency is not only committed to ensuring children are healthy, safe, enjoy and achieve in their learning, make a contribution to their community and achieve economic well-being, but do so in partnership with other children's services.

To help Early Years practitioners, teachers and others to deliver the Every Child

1

Matters outcomes this book explores aspects of the agenda from the standpoint of those training to work with children and families in an educational context, or already working in such a context and undertaking professional development. The five outcomes of the Every Child Matters agenda acknowledge that children's achievement in terms of learning is affected by other aspects of children's well-being. The government states in its *Every Child Matters: Change for children in schools* document that: 'Children can't learn if they don't feel safe or if health problems are allowed to create barriers. And education is the most effective route for young people out of poverty and disaffection' (DfES, 2004b).

In particular, in terms of providing educational provision under the Every Chid Matters agenda the government wants Early Years settings and primary schools to:

- ensure their provision is personalized to meet the needs of individual children and their families;
- build their provision in partnership with children and their families;
- offer a wide range of extended and multi-agency services;
- keep children safe and deal with bullying and other forms of discrimination;
- promote a healthy lifestyle; and
- give children a strong voice in the life of the setting or school.

Ensuring that the five outcomes of the Every Child Matters agenda are met requires that those involved in working to support children and their families understand that where a child has a challenging background, this can be overcome to enable the child to fulfil their potential (DfES, 2004b). That for some children and communities particular work needs to be done to raise awareness that education is a way out of the poverty trap. It is also recognized that settings and schools need to continue to develop their good practice in consulting with parents and families and to build even closer links with the community, if the Every Child Matters agenda is to be realized.

Most of what the Every Child Matters agenda requires of settings and primary schools has been in place for many years, however, there are aspects of practice that need to be reviewed and developed. This book aims to help Early Years practitioners, teachers and others who work with children to review aspects of their thinking and practice and to consider how their own ideas, attitudes and beliefs impact on how they approach their work with children and their families. It also explores all five outcomes of the Every Child Matters agenda in some detail, considering the wider social issues the outcomes raise and provides some practical advice about how to tackle each outcome in practice.

The single most important principle that underpins the Every Child Matters agenda is that of social justice. Chapter 1 explores what exactly is meant by social justice in the context of the Every Child Matters agenda. It examines how social justice is the principle that aims to enable everyone in society to have the opportunity to maximize their life-chances, achieve well-being and flourish. This is a principle that has been at the heart of public policy for many years, despite this there are still children and families who live in poverty and have done so for generations. To try and explore why this is so this chapter also examines what is known as *the theory of oppression*, to unpack some of the witting and unwitting discrimination that is prevalent in society and prevents some from being able to take advantage of the opportunities available to maximize their life-chances and achieve well-being.

Early Years settings and schools are expert at working with children; however, individual practitioners, teachers and others do not always mean the same thing when they talk of children, or childhood. Chapter 2 provides the opportunity for the reader to consider how society's understanding of what is meant by the term 'child' has changed over time and that what we mean personally by 'child' or 'childhood' will impact on our approach to working with children. Therefore, in exploring the notion of the child and what we can learn about being a child by listening to children, we can be sure we are better informed about the best way to support children in achieving well-being.

The Every Child Matters agenda is about children and their families and, therefore, just as meeting the agenda requires us to review our concept of what we mean by 'child', similarly it is as important to explore what we mean by family. To help the reader do this, Chapter 3 examines the notion of 'family' and good practice in working with families.

Having explored some of the wider social principles that underpin the Every Child Matters agenda the following chapters examine each outcome in more detail. Chapter 4 looks at what the Department for Children Schools and Families (DCFS) means by 'being healthy' and how settings and schools can work towards this outcome for children and families. The chapter explores what it means for children to be physically, mentally and emotionally healthy. It helps the reader to understand that healthy lifestyles include physical, mental and emotional health. In particular, the chapter explores the notion of resilience and that resilience can help children and families better achieve the five outcomes for well-being. It also provides some guidance on how the issues of sexual health and choosing not to take illegal drugs can be introduced in Early Years settings and primary schools.

Chapter 5 reviews the 'being safe' outcome and the duty that all those who come into contact with children have, in law, to ensure that children are safeguarded from maltreatment. The chapter explores what constitutes maltreatment and abuse of children. It explains how children can be vulnerable to abuse, particularly sexual abuse, and how children can be safeguarded against such abuse. The chapter also provides some ideas about how the curriculum can be used to explore these issues with children, plus guidance on the process for reporting suspected abuse and what the outcomes of reporting such incidents might be.

Early Years settings and schools have considerable experience and success in enabling children to enjoy and achieve in their learning. For this reason, having explored different models of children's learning, Chapter 6 looks particularly at the concept and practice of personalized learning and Assessment for Learning and how these aspects of prioritized educational practice can enable children to enjoy and achieve.

Chapter 7 explores the fourth Every Child Matters outcome, that of how children and families can be enabled to 'make a positive contribution'. In examining this outcome the chapter investigates how children can be given a voice in the decisions-making processes in settings and schools. It also explores how giving children a voice helps protect them against discrimination and helps them to develop self-confidence and deal with life-challenges, particularly at important transition points in their lives.

The final chapter of the book looks at the last of the five outcomes, that of enjoying economic well-being. In exploring this concept in Chapter 8, the book examines factors that militate against economic well-being including poverty, race and class. It investigates how, with appropriate family support, children can be better enabled to achieve economic well-being and how extended services can help children and families achieve economic well-being.

Every Child Matters and the Social Justice Agenda

The principles of how everyone can achieve equitable access to the goods available in society, for example, housing, food, health and education, is a concern that has long occupied humanity. Social justice is a principle that is currently used in Britain to underpin public policy and practice with a view to ensuring all have an equal chance to attain the necessary goods and conditions they need to thrive and achieve well-being. Embedded in the concept of social justice is the idea of *fairness* (DfES, 2005: 21), that is, in a fair society all should have an equal chance of achieving well-being. However, society is not a homogenous entity. It comprises a huge number of smaller groups between which is an unequal distribution of power and access to goods, and as part of the unequal power distribution some groups will wittingly – or unwittingly – discriminate against others. In this way, some are prevented from being able to achieve well-being.

The Every Child Matters agenda, through its five outcomes for well-being seeks, underpinned by social justice, to ensure children and families are supported in achieving health, safety, enjoyment of and achievement in learning, and that they can play their part in the community and achieve economic well-being. While these outcomes can be recognized for children and families in the short term, in some cases with considerable support from others, the goal of the ECM agenda is to provide children and families with the long-term skills, knowledge and understanding to be able to achieve these outcomes for themselves. And, if as individuals we have a concern in helping children and families achieve these goals, we need to be clear about the principles that underpin the ECM agenda to ensure we are best equipped to be working to see it realized. For these reasons, this chapter begins with unpacking what is meant by social justice, as understanding this is fundamental to being clear about how to approach the rest of the ECM agenda.

What is social justice?

Most of us are familiar with the notion of justice and use a very sound working knowledge of it in our day-to-day lives. However, given time to think through exactly what we might mean by justice, it quickly becomes evident that it is not one thing, but that there are a number of aspects to the concept of justice.

In Western Europe it is usually the Ancient Greek philosopher Plato (424–347 BCE), who is credited with first exploring justice and establishing our current uses of the term (Hinman, 2003: 243). From Plato we have derived the notion that justice is a good thing for society, that we should seek to be able to call ourselves a 'just' society and that a just society is something of value and is worth striving for (Hinman, 2003: 245). The absolute definition of the concept of justice is still under discussion – nearly 2400 years later – but generally when we talk of justice two principle things we expect from it are what we might call retributive justice and distributive justice.

- Retributive justice is the term applied to the notion of imposing a penalty, sometimes a punishment for the breaking of an agreed rule or a law.
- Distributive justice is about how a 'just' society might share or distribute limited, but necessary, things that everyone needs to thrive (De Botton, 2001: 94; Graham, 2007: 15; Hinman, 2003: 249).

There are other aspects to justice that could be explored: restorative justice, for example, which rather than being concerned with punishment as in retributive justice, has more to do with re-establishing harmony, perhaps in a society that has experienced some form of civil unrest, possibly including acts of oppression by one group against another (Hinman, 2003: 257). There are also concepts of 'natural' justice and the notion of a just reward; in both these aspects of justice there is the implication that there is some natural order outside human political constructs and rules that would seem to govern what is just in certain instances, over and above what human rules might state. In terms of the concept of social justice, it is the principle of distributive justice that we are most engaged with.

Distributive justice is concerned with how a society 'in which everything currently and conventionally regarded as a benefit or an advantage is freely available to all' (Boucher, 1998: 255). In Britain it has become the case that the government is the main agent for ensuring that benefits and advantages are accessible to all and that they are fairly distributed (Boucher, 1998). However, in distributing goods, the agency undertaking the distribution is faced with resolving two important issues:

1. How do we know how much of each of these benefits and advantages any one person should have?
2. Were we to start from a position where there is already an unequal distribution of these benefits and advantages – where some people seems to have none and others have them in abundance – what processes do we use to even things out?

The answer to the first question is usually tackled in terms of establishing a notion of a *minimum* of, for example, housing, food, health and education that an individual needs to survive (Boucher, 1998: 256), and that it is the minimum that everyone is entitled to so that they are kept from living in poverty. (Poverty is discussed in more detail in Chapter 8.) However, finding a distribution method – or possibly even a *re*distribution method to ensure all have an equal chance to enjoy the benefits and advantages a society has to offer – is a considerable challenge and the rest of this chapter explores how social justice seeks to provide a way forward in meeting this challenge.

Well-being and flourishing

Boucher (1998), in exploring the notion of what a minimum of benefits and advantages might be, also reminds us that as a society we are not just concerned with physical well-being, the need for food, shelter and health care, but also with what might constitute 'the minimum conditions for the promotion of self-realization' (Boucher, 1998: 83).

The notion that human self-realization or well-being ought to be as important for human flourishing as having access to the basics for survival is one that, in Europe, was explored by Aristotle (384 BC–322 BCE) and stills continues to exercise us. More recently it is the work of psychologist Abraham Maslow who is central to the discussion that human experience ought to be about more than simply having the means to survive. Writing in the 1950s, Maslow developed what has become known as 'Maslow's hierarchy of needs'. This notion is usually expressed diagrammatically in the form of a pyramid. At the base of the pyramid, the pyramid's widest part, Maslow places the basic needs human beings have, those that must be met in order for them simply to survive, for example, food, drink, shelter, warmth, and so on. As we move up the pyramid and the pyramid narrows, then the needs identified by Maslow move through the need to be safe, to belong, be loved and have friends, through to esteem needs. At the very top of the pyramid is what Maslow calls 'self-actualization', or personal growth and fulfilment. The notion of the pyramid is particularly powerful, since it also represents how, as we move 'up' the pyramid from basic needs to self-actualization, the access to the goods or conditions we need to help us achieve self-actualization becomes narrower, or more restricted (Plummer, 2005: 18). Some have questioned that in order to live human beings need to be self-actualized at all. However, while the need for food and drink is self-evident in terms of survival, Maslow argues that self-actualization is also crucial to the flourishing of the individual and to society in general. Self-actualization is about how the individual sees themselves, and what 'the person sees' will enable or prevent not only their own flourishing but how they will function in relation to others (Freiberg, 1999: 4).

Therefore, in seeking to distribute societal advantages and benefits we are not only concerned with a minimum level of existence, but also with what individuals need, overall, to thrive. Human flourishing is not only about the basics needed to survive, it is also influenced by an individual's access to an education which enables enjoyment and achievement, including enjoying a sense of personal safety, being able to contribute to the community and having the means to achieve personal and long-term economic well-being; indeed, all the outcomes of the Every Child Matters agenda.

The welfare state

In Britain there has long been a concern for how best to provide the conditions for everyone to flourish. In effect the roots of social justice, although called by another name, can be found in laws that date from the seventeenth century. Laws that state how the poor are to be provided for, or 'Poor Laws', first appeared in 1598 (Social Policy in the UK, 2008). Further Poor Laws, for example that of 1601, placed the duty on church parishes to levy a 'compulsory poor rate', ensure the appointment of '"overseers" of relief' and ensure that there was *provision for* 'setting the poor on work' (Social Policy in the UK, 2008), all of which are principles we recognize as still being part of the current welfare system.

The mechanisms by which we currently seek to achieve universal flourishing, and that, in part it is the government's responsibility to ensure this happens, began to emerge in the 1940s (Lund, 2002: 1). In 1942 the idea of what has become the welfare state was first outlined in the Beveridge Report (Lund, 2002: 107) and from 1948 onward began to take the shape we recognize now such that we now expect the welfare state to provide the following:

- social security (money for those who are currently unemployed or unable to work);
- free health care at the point of need;
- affordable housing for all;
- free education; and
- other free welfare services for children (Lund, 2002: 107; Social Policy in the UK, 2008).

These ideas began to be explored at the end of the nineteenth century, mainly through the influence of a group that became known as the 'British Idealists' (Boucher, 1998: 83; Lund, 2002: 1). Over time, their exploration of how goods should be shared and, in particular, provided for those who seem not to have ready access to enough goods to flourish, has formed the principles of subsequent governments' welfare policies (Lund, 2002). What is new about using the ECM agenda to tackle theses issues, compared with other government welfare polices, is that while it is recognized that it may be necessary, in some instances, to *give* goods to children and families, the long-term objective is that, through education and other multi-agency support, children and families can develop their own capacities to provide these goods for themselves. That is, with the appropriate initial support, children will grow up with the skills, knowledge and understanding of how to:

- maintain their own health – through adopting a healthy lifestyle;
- keep themselves safe – in the broadest sense;
- achieve economic well-being and contribute to the community.

Importantly for all who work or intend to work with children and their families, in Early Years settings or schools, central to the success of the ECM agenda is that children enjoy learning and achieve in their learning across all phases of education, from the very early years onwards, since this is where the foundations for long-term well-being and the achievement of all the outcomes are set.

Traditionally, in British politics these notions of welfare policy and social justice have seemed to sit more comfortably in the socialist, or 'left-wing', tenets of welfare policy principles, where 'socialism is perhaps the ancestor' (Boucher, 1998: 255) of these ideas. Indeed the ECM agenda is a Labour government policy. However, social justice is now seen as an integral principle of both main political parties' welfare policies and this was signalled in 2005 by the Conservative Party when they too pledged their commitment to pursuing welfare through the principles of social justice. In a press release they acknowledged that their approach to dealing with the 'causes and consequences of poverty in Britain' would be through measures that 'empower the least well-off to climb the ladder from poverty to wealth' and that this would be through an approach that applied the principles of 'social justice' (BBC, 2005b).

Life-chances

What continues to exercise those concerned with social justice is that, despite these seemingly considerable advances in providing equal access to the goods discussed, we still live in a society that has families living in poverty, and for some families this seems to happen generation after generation. In understanding why this continues to happen, we need to consider how access to goods has actually been managed and controlled.

One of the most influential theorists in this field is John Rawls (Graham, 2007). Rawls was concerned to explore, not only the rules by which goods might be divided up between members of a society, but the factors that impact on deciding those rules and who makes the rules in the first instance. For example, he was aware of how important 'luck' seemed to be in enabling persons to thrive, the 'luck' that comes with being born into particular groups in society, groups that then make for better life-chances than others. And 'Rawls was acutely aware of the extent to which' luck is not deserved – it is 'simply luck' (Hinman, 2003: 245). That is, should our chances of flourishing and achieving well-being be determined only by accident – something that we have no control over? As a sophisticated civilized society, surely we ought to be able to establish a way of ensuring factors that are under our control can be used to better our life-chances, so that we can be active agents in the process and not simply have to rely on something as arbitrary as accident of birth. Through his work, Rawls examined how inequalities of birth impact on life-chances and perpetuate injustices in society, particularly those linked to the race, class or religion a person may be born into. He explored how these injustices occasioned by birth might be mitigated against, so we might create a just society in which luck plays a minimal role in enabling individuals to thrive (Hinman, 2003: 245). Rawls explored the notion of writing principles – or what he termed 'rules' – for the distributing or redistributing of goods through what he called the 'veil of ignorance' (Hinman, 2003: 246). That is, if we were to write the rules for the distribution of goods, without knowing what our position in society is to be, for example, the family we are to be born into, we may find that we have very different notions of what the rules should be when we do discover who our family is and how those rules actually impact on us.

Activity

You are writing the rules that govern 'going on holiday', write five principles, or rules that you believe every holiday should be based on.

You have written these principles behind the *veil of ignorance*. Now consider the following, you are a member of a family of five, and in your family there are two working adults – a man and a woman who are partners and parents of a 15-year-old boy and a 7-year-old girl – and there is an 85-year-old man, who is the father

continued

continued

of one of the adults, living with them. How do your rules work in deciding about this family's holiday?

Now imagine that the family have an annual income of £27,000 and that the maximum they can spend on the holiday is £1,500 – how does that affect your principles about the holidaying?

Now imagine what holiday you might want from the point of view of each member of the family. Go back to your original list of principles, how have they changed?

The social justice theory of oppression

It can be argued that, leaving luck aside, British society already provides considerable equal access to all benefits and advantages needed to thrive. A child might be born into a household that is impoverished in terms of food and housing, but society will provide it with access to health care and education and through these benefits the child has the opportunity to move from poverty into a more flourishing life. However, there are other theorists of social justice who claim that this is not the case since there are other factors at work, besides luck of birth, that mitigate against individuals being able to flourish, these factors are discussed in the next section through exploring the concept of the *theory of oppression*.

In discussing the benefits and advantages children and families need to thrive and flourish we have concentrated on tangible things. Things that exist in a physical form and can be given to, or acquired by, others. Theorists of social justice claim that there are factors that impact on the likelihood of individual flourishing that are as influential to life-outcomes, but are far less tangible and therefore more difficult to distribute between those that have and those that are impoverished. Rawls explores these intangible benefits and advantages in terms of how they are linked to the race and class individuals are born into (Hinman, 2003: 245), and these factors generally in social justice theories of oppression are seen as being defining factors in impacting on an individuals life-chances. We know that there are inequalities between families in terms of the level of material goods and wealth they have (Wissenberg, 1999), but it is also the case that inequalities exist between the cultural groups that we are born into, whether we define these groups by ethnicity, religion or class. Within British society, the cultural group that a child is born into will determine the level of success the child will have in accessing the advantages and benefits available. This is not necessarily because these goods will not be, in theory, available to all children, but because, in reality, the attitudes and beliefs held by some groups in society prevent all groups from being able to successfully access them.

As proponents of the theory of oppression Adams et al. (2007), explore how some groups in British society hold more economic and cultural power than others, and it is most often these groups that also have the control over goods and how these goods are distributed. What is under scrutiny here is not the actual dividing up of the goods, but the way in which the values, beliefs and attitudes of those in a position to divide up the goods, prevent this from happening. That is, either deliberately or unwittingly, some groups oppress others and prevent them from making the most of the life-chances available. 'We use the term oppression rather than discrimination, bias, prejudice, or bigotry to emphasise the pervasive nature of social inequality woven throughout social institutions as well as embedded within individual consciousness' (Adams et al., 2007: 3).

We are all members of a range of groups, each with a set of beliefs, values and attitudes that bind the group together. In any one day, we will pass in and out of a number of groups. Sometimes we are in groups that are being oppressed by others and sometimes we are the oppressors. That we are being oppressed or are oppressors is often invisible to us, unless it is brought to our attention. In our own homes we might have quite a lot of power, particularly over certain elements of what happens there; other aspects of home life we have to negotiate. At work, or when we go out into society, we may have to do what others tell us – or we may be in a position of authority and tell others what to do – again, this might involve some negotiation. When we are with our friends we may feel we are with a group where the power is fairly evenly distributed – and, indeed, for many these are the groups from which they derive the greatest sense of well-being. Besides these small groups we are members of, we are also part of wider societal groups, for example, we can be grouped by gender, ethnicity, religion and class, and often there are inequalities in power relationships between these groups, which may or may not affect our ability to access the benefits and advantages on offer and our capacity to achieve long-term well-being.

Social justice is concerned with exploring the power that different groups have, both at local and national levels and how the values attitudes and beliefs that bind the members of groups together cause them to exercise oppressive power over other groups. 'Oppression not only resides in external social institutions and norms but lodges in the human psyche as well', and not only this, 'but oppressive beliefs are internalized by victims as well as perpetrators' (Adams et al., 2007: 4).

That is, for us to have a truly equal society, not only must we recognize when we are being oppressed, but when we are oppressing too. Oppression is an important concept to understand and reflect on, since it not only affects the way we behave towards others, but it also 'restricts both self-development and self-determination' (Adams et al., 2007: 3). Oppression happens in this way because we are not lone individuals, we live as members of groups and communities and 'our identities are fundamentally constructed in relation to others and to the cultures in which we are embedded' (Adams et al., 2007: 9). We take on the values, beliefs and attitudes of those around us, and our actions are influenced by these attitudes and beliefs, however inadvertently, and have an impact, positively or negatively, on the lives of others. Most people wish to have a positive impact on the lives of others, particularly those who work or intend to work with children and families. The problem here is that we may be making assumptions, based only on our beliefs, that what we are doing is best for others, so we need to examine very carefully just where we got our beliefs and attitudes from, and what our evidence is for knowing they are correct, before we use them as our only guide to managing the lives of others.

That we are complicit in the ongoing situation of oppression, in terms of how we allow ourselves to be oppressed and continue to oppress others, is explored by Gramsci's notion of hegemony whereby Gramsci suggests: 'a dominant group can so successfully project its particular way of seeing social reality that its view is accepted as common sense, as part of the natural order, even by those who are disempowered by it' (Adams et al., 2007: 10). That such a state of affairs can happen is possible because, as the idea of hegemony explains, we all live in complex relationships, one with another. And power is not necessarily always imposed by one group onto another; power tensions can exist within groups, too. Therefore, whatever the values, attitudes and beliefs of one, or a few, dominant persons in a group can become – if other members of the group allow it to happen – the dominant discourse for that group.

Part of what causes the tension and oppressive practices within and between groups is the notion of privilege. Specifically, some groups or individuals are, for whatever reasons, advantaged and they are the ones who determine what comes to regarded as 'normal' in terms of values, attitudes and beliefs. Tensions also occur where groups act as if what are their own values, attitudes and beliefs are 'normal' not only for themselves, but for everyone else too and try to makes their views the prevailing view. Another way of expressing this idea is through the concept of dominant discourses, that is, what advantaged groups decide is the norm in terms of values, attitudes and beliefs becomes the dominant view or discourse through which all notions of correct and incorrect ideas are debated – and those that are deemed incorrect notions, views or individuals are marginalized. The activity below is an example of how the media, in particular, is a strong mouthpiece for those who want to perpetuate and further normalize particular dominant discourses.

Activity

In September 2006 the *Telegraph* newspaper ran an article entitled 'Mrs Chips takes orders for the school dinners run' about a group of mothers who were 'delivering fast food through a school's fence' to their children and the children of other families. They were described as 'using a supermarket trolley to make daily runs with fish and chips, pies, burgers, sandwiches and fizzy drinks from local takeaways'. The paper claimed that the parents were 'taking action because pupils are turning up their noses at what they describe as "overpriced, low-fat rubbish"'.

continued

continued

The newspaper also suggested that local environmental health and educational officials had been contacted to establish whether this was actually hygienically safe and if the parents might require a licence to distribute food in this way. It was stated that 50 to 60 meals were being distributed to children in this way, each day. One of the mothers was quoted as saying: 'Food is cheaper and better at the local takeaways ... We just want to make sure the kids are properly fed. They don't enjoy the school food and the end result is that they are starving.'

The school claimed it was trying to serve 'healthier' foods, with increased opportunity to buy and eat fruit and vegetables and less fried food on offer. The head teacher was quote as saying: 'I'm stunned. What these two women are doing is unbelievable ... these mums want to effectively shorten the lives of their kids' (Stokes, 2006).

Having read this article:

- What do you think about the mothers' behaviour?
- Which particularly aspects of the article make you think in this way?

Now compare what you have just read with some quotes from the BBC's reporting of the same incident, and as you read them, think carefully about the language being used to report the incident.

The BBC article was headlined 'School dinner row meeting held', and here is a direct quote: 'Parents who are opposed to the introduction of healthy meals at a South Yorkshire school have held a meeting with its deputy head teacher. Some parents of Rawmarsh Comprehensive pupils have been taking orders for fish and chips and delivering it through the fence at the Rotherham school.'

The BBC states that the parents felt they needed to do this because the children were not being given enough time to eat their meals, or enough choice in what was being served. They also said the children did not like the quality of the food. And the BBC reports the same mother as quoted in the newspaper article above as saying: 'she was receiving orders for healthy jacket potatoes and salad sandwiches as well as burgers and fish and chips'. The head teacher is quoted as saying he would meet with the parents and that he saw 'the dialogue as it stands is really in terms of us persuading them of the effectiveness of the strategy we have put in place' (BBC, 2006).

- Have your feelings about the mothers changed by reading a different version of events?

Also compare what actual words are used in both articles, in the *Telegraph*'s version of the event, the parents are reported to use words like 'kids' and 'overpriced, low-fat rubbish', they turn up at the fence (not at the front gate, or in reception) with a supermarket trolley full of fish and chips, pies, burgers, sandwiches and fizzy drinks from local takeaways, while the school's concern is only for the health and safety of the children. How is the BBC's use of language different in their report of the event?

- Having compared the two versions of events, what can we learn about how the press can influence our views of ideas and events?

The issues raised by the theory of oppression are challenging to deal with, since they require us to reflect on those attitudes, beliefs and values that make up the very fabric of who we are. However, if we do not make some attempt to explore what we believe to be the case and what evidence we have for knowing we are correct, then we may be in danger of blindly accepting conditions under which we continue to oppress others, and allow ourselves to be oppressed, since we regard this as the normal and unchanging state of affairs (Adams et al., 2007: 11).

It is very hard to challenge accepted norms not only because of the personal internal conflict and uncertainty it can cause, but also because other members of our groups might also challenge us or act with antagonism towards us. We often see this in groups, whether family groups, social groups or those we work or study with; there is often conflict when someone suggests a change in practice, or simply suggests doing something differently, even seemingly very minor things. Sometimes the suggestions for change comes from a group member, but more usually, particularly where we are concerned with wider issues of oppression, it is those who perceive themselves as being most oppressed who have the most to gain from trying to change things. In many instances this causes the greatest conflict as the oppressing group(s) may have the most incentive to maintain things as they are.

Activity

Think of the different groups you belong to and a time when you wanted to change something about the way the group went about things. Perhaps it was something as simple as wanting to move the furniture around in the bedroom, or to do with changing a process at work, or deciding what to do as a social event for a group of friends.

Did you manage to make the changes you wanted?
Did you encounter any opposition to your ideas?
How did you deal with that opposition?
If you could not make the changes you wanted, why was that?
How was your change prevented from happening?
How has the episode left you feeling?
Will you give up on the change, or try again?

The groups we have most contact with, particularly as we are growing up, will have a considerable formative impact on our sense of self, our values, attitudes and beliefs. While this may not be of too much significance in day-to-day terms, it becomes more important to consider what values attitudes and beliefs we are drawing on when we are working with children and their families, particularly if we are in a position where we have the power to make our beliefs and attitudes the dominant discourse – or at least behave if our understandings and assumptions are those that are held by everyone and understood by everyone. What we need to be aware of in all our work with children and their families is the *inequalities of social status* and *social position*, including the *differences in cultural contexts* that may exist between us, in our settings and schools and the children and families we are seeking to support. We need to be aware of the ways 'in which oppression and cultural context together' may lead to possible tensions between setting and schools and families, possibly, with the children caught in the middle (Adams et al., 2007: 17). Social justice is not about moving power from the oppressing group to the oppressed; it is about both groups, oppressed and oppressors working together to share power and goods in a way that benefits everyone concerned.

The ECM agenda seeks to provide for all children, young people and their families to achieve the five outcomes for well-being. Early years settings and primary schools are central to enabling this to happen, but if we are to fully understand our role in ensuring the ECM agenda provides what is intended for children and their families, we need to be clear about our own position in the hierarchy of oppression. If we do not listen to what others are saying about the support they need and how best they can access it and simply continue on as we have always done, then we will fail to connect with countless children and their families and be unable to realize the ECM agenda for them. It may come as a shock to consider ourselves as 'being oppressors', as we may actually think of ourselves as helping others, but we cannot do this unless we consult with others and act upon what they have to say. The principle is to work with children and families, not to make assumptions about what is best for them – neither is it expected that consultation means the management and organization of the setting or school will be 'handed over' to them.

Let us briefly consider the way settings and schools are organized, for example, generally the practitioners and teachers, led by the setting manager or head teacher and senior management team, make the decisions about how the organization is to be run – the level of input other people have in these decisions will vary from organization to organization. These decisions, often in the form of policy and practice are then passed on to others who are involved in the day-to-day running of the organization and in planning and undertaking the learning activities and processes that actually take place. It has been the dominant discourse that only those who hold recognized professional qualifications can be in the advantaged group that has the last say in decision-making and what information is passed on to others. However, Every Child Matters requires Early Years settings and schools to reflect on this position and work with the children, families and others involved in the organization, and to actively consult with them to ensure the settings and schools are meeting actual needs in appropriate ways, not simply making assumptions about needs or about how best to meet them.

To further explore how these dominant discourses, perpetuated by those in positions of advantage, can marginalize the very groups they are trying to help, let us take as an example the process of reading and learning to read. Settings and schools invest a lot of their resources, time, effort and money in encouraging children and families to become involved in reading. Both the Early Years Foundation Stage framework and the National Curriculum are considerably focused on the processes and support children's need to become fluent readers and to read for pleasure as well as for practical reasons. By the time children reach primary school the National Curriculum states that children should read a range of literature that includes: 'stories, plays and poems by significant children's authors and: a range of modern fiction by significant children's authors and long-established children's fiction' (DfEE/QCA, 1999: 47/54). Research shows that teachers interpret this as being a fairly traditional diet of British 'classic' fiction texts and poems, and contemporary authors that reflect the teachers' background and 'interests with teachers relying on the same texts over a lengthy period' (OfSTED, 2005b). The research also shows that teachers' interpretation of the literature aspect of the National Curriculum reading programme of study does not reflect children's interests and encourage children to read for pleasure outside school (OfSTED, 2005b; 2005c). Indeed there is a 'dissonance between school reading and home reading choices and experiences' (OfSTED, 2005b: 9). Where children are given the opportunity to talk about what does influence what they read, most children cited friends as influences on their reading choices; 'fewer pupils mentioned that their reading had been influenced greatly by teachers' (OfSTED, 2005b: 24). Furthermore, those children who most experience this dissonance are boys and particularly boys from socio-economically disadvantaged backgrounds and ethnic minorities (OfSTED, 2005b; 2005c). This research (OfSTED, 2005b; 2005c) into children's reading habits showed that both boys and girls enjoyed reading comics and multi-modal texts for pleasure, neither of which are routinely used by many schools to engage children in reading; indeed, the children themselves said they thought teachers did not approve of comics (OfSTED, 2005b: 9). Here we have a good example of the dominant group – the teachers, deciding what it is best to use to encourage children to read and the subordinate group – or the oppressed group having what will actually encourage them to read at best ignored and at worst actively disapproved of. Comics are not inherently bad, and as a way of motivating children to read might be shown to be good. Yet unless the notion that it is wrong to let children read comics at school is challenged they will continue to be seen as bad and the dissonance between home and school, in terms of reading, for certain children, will continue to be there. The school's notion of what it is correct to read oppresses the home notion and in this way undermines the self-esteem of the child and family, who will learn to 'accept and incorporate negative images of themselves fostered by the dominant society' (Adams et al., 2007: 11) and the child cannot flourish in school and enjoy and achieve, if they believe the school denigrates what they and their family enjoy.

The reading example above is only one of many instances of how settings and schools have, in the past, used their position of privilege – in being the mouthpiece for unchallenged dominant discourses, to continue to oppress certain groups in society, both through the language they use in communicating with children and parents and in their practices (Adams et al., 2007: 12). For example, in the 1970s and into the 1980s children for whom English was an Additional Language (EAL) were not 'allowed' to speak in anything other than English at school (Knowles, 2006: 61). For young children coming into school in Reception, an experience that was already challenging for some young children, to then be denied a language to communicate in and make friends with, further isolated the child. The same applied to older children who might be new to Britain and joined a school later in the primary phase. Without access to language to explain their needs, thoughts and feelings – or to talk to their friends – these children, now adults, speak of the fear and isolation they felt as children (Knowles, 2006: 61). Writing about her experiences of being a young Sikh girl new to Britain in the 1970s, the black educationalist and writer Vini Lander writes:

> Immigrant children were not encouraged to maintain their mother tongue, the prevailing view being that it would impede the acquisition of English. As a child at that time, I remember my parents 'buying into' this and telling me to speak English at home. This was at the expense of reduced proficiency in Punjabi. I now speak Punjabi at a basic level but I am not literate in my mother tongue (Knowles, 2006: 61).

While policy and practice with regard to children for whom English is an additional language has moved on considerably since then, what is important to reflect on here is, the long-term harm done to all those children who were denied a language and how oppressed groups will accept the dominant discourses even to their own harm and disadvantage.

Case study

This case study considers the importance of listening to the child's voice as one that can be potentially oppressed to the point of being silenced.

A teaching assistant in a school on the coastal strip of south-east England had been given the responsibility of helping EAL children new to the school to settle in. Until recently the school had been mainly 'all white' and was working hard to find ways to support the increasing numbers of Eastern European children joining the school whose first language was not English.

In reviewing the successes or otherwise of the school's practices the teaching assistant (TA) decided to talk to some of the children from Bulgaria and Poland and ask them about what had worked for them in terms of helping them settle into school, and what needed to be different for new children in the future.

Not only did the activity raise the self-esteem of the children, it also uncovered some huge gaps in the school's provision. The children said nobody showed them around the school, they did not know where the toilets were, they did not know who all the adults were – who was the head teacher, who were the teachers, teaching assistants and lunchtime supervisors – and they did not understand registration – they thought their names were being called because they had been naughty. They were convinced they had done something terrible when their name was read out in assembly from the 'golden book'.

From this experience, the school has developed a colour booklet and welcome pack for EAL children, available in a number of languages, so parents can talk through with their children what happens at school. The school has also developed a system for training children to 'buddy' other children new to the school.

While many settings and schools have made huge strides in listening to children and families and finding ways to build supportive, reciprocal relationships with each other, rather than the setting or school taking the lead at all times, there is still a way to go before true partnerships are established. Many settings and schools are still guilty of sending home information that presupposes those receiving it can read, can read the information in the language it is written in and understand the terminology being used. To continue the reading example, many settings and schools send home information about the importance of reading to children, with children and listening to the children themselves read. Sometimes the information can use quite technical terms, for example, phonics, phoneme, Early Years Foundation Stage, National Curriculum, programme of study, level of achievement. Even terms which seem quite common and obvious to those who deal with them every day, like fiction, non-fiction, story books or sharing a book, may be alien terms to other groups. Therefore, by using only the terminology of the group 'in charge', other, more marginalized, groups can be made to feel inferior if they do not know what these terms mean. Even if the setting or school puts on events to explain these terms and to model what is meant by some of them, they need to give consideration to when parents can actually come to such meetings and how are they going to deal sensitively with those parents who cannot read.

Activity

Hopefully what you have read so far has caused you to reflect on some of your own values, attitudes and beliefs, and where you have collected them from and how you operate with them in your relationships with others – or how you let them influence what you are prepared to accept in terms of others' behaviours towards you. Beginning to think through where we have 'come from' and how we unthinkingly fall back on our values, attitudes and beliefs in our day-to-day lives can be quite a challenging experience. Using some of the starting points below, you can begin to reflect on what you believe, what values and attitudes you hold, and how comfortable you feel with them.

Personal journey maps – draw a 'map' of your personal journey that shows how you have arrived at where you are today. 'Signpost' those things that helped you on your journey and those things that 'got in the way'. Try to identify particular events, times and places in your map, when you met particular people who had a strong influence on who you are today. Are there any times in your life where particular people or events significantly changed the way you looked at things?

Stopping and thinking about your own values, attitudes and beliefs – the next time you are going to share your views on something, or give and opinion, think, why do I believe that/how do I know I am correct? Do I have anything to 'back up' my views?

Trying out others' suggestions – the next time somebody suggests doing something differently, try going along with them, even if you have some reservations. If this is too challenging, say 'OK, we'll try that, but if I don't like it, or it is isn't working for me, I reserve the right to stop doing it'.

continued

continued

You might also like to try some of the ideas below

Looking at things from different points of view – try reading newspapers you do not usually buy, or watching television programmes on topics and channels that you had not previously considered watching (including international programmes, if you can). What do you notice about the different ways the same incidents are reported?

Visit the BBC voices website – personal stories and accounts can be very powerful in making us think about things in a different way. The website, www.bbc.co.uk/voices/, contains personal stories from all sorts of people, across all aspects of society. Try visiting the website and listening to some of the stories, perhaps those told by people you do not have the opportunity to meet in your day-to-day life. See how their experiences have influenced their attitudes, values and beliefs; what are the similarities and differences between your story and theirs?

Social justice in the statutory framework for the Early Years Foundation Stage and the National Curriculum

Not only is the ECM agenda underpinned by the notion of social justice, but it is also a requirement that children are taught the principles of the concept too. The Statutory Framework for the Early Years Foundation Stage (EYFS) and the National Curriculum (NC) do not mention the notion of social justice by name. However, the principles that underpin both documents and aspects of the learning areas and subjects they cover are, in essence, those which explore social justice issues. The subjects most specifically related to tackling social justice issues are those of personal, social and emotional development and citizenship, all of which occur by name or in some form in the EYFS and the NC. Further to this, since the notion of social justice has come to be more widely discussed in society, the then Department for Education and Skills (DfES) – now the Department for Children, Families and Schools – has published additional curriculum guidance for Early Years (EY) settings and schools, which does use the term social justice, for example, the DfES (2005) document *Developing the Global Dimension in the School Curriculum.*

In exploring social justice as a principle of the NC, *Developing the Global Dimension in the School Curriculum* states:

> 'Education influences and reflects the values of society, and the kind of society we want to be ... Education is ... a route to equality of opportunity for all, a healthy and just democracy, a productive economy, and sustainable development. Education should reflect the enduring values that contribute to these ends. These include valuing ... the wider groups to which we belong, the diversity in our society and the environment in which we live. (DfES, 2005: 6)

The document goes on to explore for Early Years practitioners and teachers how one of the principles that underpins the EYFS framework is one that helps children work towards understanding 'social justice' (DfES, 2005: 4). It states, children should begin to understand the concept of social justice as it is about:

- understanding the importance of equality, justice and fairness for all within and between societies;
- recognising the impact of unequal power and access to resources;
- appreciating that actions have both intended and unintended consequences on people's lives and appreciating the importance of informed choices;
- developing the motivation and commitment to take action that will contribute to a more just world;
- challenging racism and other forms of discrimination, inequality and injustice. (DfES, 2005: 21)

The document discusses ways in which children in the EY, and then through the primary years, can be introduced to the concept of social justice and associated issues can be explored through day-to-day learning activities. Some of the ideas present in the document are outlined in the activities below.

Activity

Teaching social justice in the early years

In encouraging very young children to begin to engage with the concept of social justice, the DfES suggests that young children can begin to explore their 'relationships to others to the different communities that they are part of, for example, family, setting, school and other groups and activities they might be part of'. And through this they 'begin to develop an awareness of the diversity of peoples, places, cultures, languages and religions. They begin to understand fairness, the need to care for other people and the environment, and to be sensitive to the needs of others' (DFES, 2005: 9).

If you are keen to try some of these ideas, a place to start might be through a personal, social and emotional development learning activity, or though a communication, language and literacy activity where:

- Children consider people in particular situations and whether they might be happy, sad, hungry or lonely – using pictures and photographs.
- Children look at photos of other children from around the world and discuss what needs we all share such as the need for love, a home, friends, food, water, security and shelter.
- Children listen to and talk about stories from around the world on topics such as fairness and the environment. (DfES, 2005: 10)

Activity

Teaching social justice in the primary phase (5–11 years of age)

As children grow-up they deepen their understanding of their own sense of self and how they have a part to play in the wider world. They learn that everyone has the same basic needs, but that there are differences in the way that these needs are met. They deepen their understanding about the similarities and differences between people and places around the world 'and about disparities in the world. They develop their sense of social justice and moral responsibility and begin to understand that their own choices can affect global issues, as well as local ones' (DfES, 2005: 9)

Activities you might try with children between the ages of 5 and 7 could be a literacy activity that provides the opportunity for children to engage in speaking and listening activities, discussing fiction or non-fiction texts 'about people, places and cultures in other countries' (DfES, 2005: 10), exploring ideas of similarities and differences in lifestyle and culture. For example, by saying:

'Now we have read about X let's think about Y:
What do we do/have, that X does/has too?
What do we play with/visit, that X does?
What things do we like that X does?
What things are different about X's life and our lives?
Why do you think things are different in Z for X?'

An activity to try with older children (8–11) in a literacy session, might be around reading: 'stories, poetry and texts drawn from a variety of cultures and traditions such as diaries, autobiographies, newspapers and magazines, all of which can include the global dimension' (DfES, 2005: 11). Again, through well-focused speaking and listening activities, including group discussion and drama, the children can be encouraged to 'engage in discussions and debates about topical issues and use drama to explore the experiences of others' (DfES, 2005: 11).

Further reading

Department for Education and Skills (DfES) (2003) *Sustainable development action plan for education and skills*. London: DfES.

Department for Education and Skills (DfES) (2004) *Putting the world into world-class education: an international strategy for education, skills and children's services.* (DfES/1077/2004).

Department for Education and Skills (DfES) (2004) *Working together: giving children and young people a say.* (DfES/0134/2004).

Department for Children, Schools and Families (DCSF) (2008) *Working together: listening to the voices of children and young people.* DCSF/00410/2008.

Useful websites

www.oxfam.org.uk/coolplanet/teachers/catalogue.htm

www.unicef.org.uk/teacherzone

www.dfid.gov.uk

www.citizenship-global.org.uk

www.geography.org.uk/global

www.globaldimension.org.uk

www.qca.org.uk/respectforall

2

The Child in Society

This chapter explores:

- how society's understanding of what is meant by the term 'child' has changed over time;
- what we mean by the notion of 'childhood';
- how different agencies working to support children and their families use different models of the child;
- how the Every Child Matters agenda requires tensions between agencies to be resolved; and
- how the Every Child Matters agenda requires the voice of the child to be at the centre of the agenda.

While education is concerned with learning and academic achievement, it is also very concerned with enabling children to explore and develop social, performance and physical skills. Early Years settings and schools have in turn increasingly realized that developing these skills and helping children to learn needs to be done in partnership with the child's home and family. Since, when a child comes to the Early Years setting or into school, the family come too, the beliefs and values held by the family come with the child; they are not left at the door. However, under the ECM agenda, settings and schools are now required to be even more proactive in listening to and working with children and their families to develop provision and to work closely with other agencies also working to support children and their families. For both these aspects of the ECM agenda to be successful, it is helpful for settings and schools to reflect on what model of the child they consciously – or subconsciously – use, as they go about their day-to-day business, and how that model helps – or hinders – their relationship with the child's parents and with other agencies. This chapter seeks to explore how dominant discourses with regard to what society views children as being have changed over time, what current models of the child are prevalent in different sectors in society and how these impact on the child's experience of 'being a child' and childhood.

How society's understanding of what is meant by the term 'child' has changed over time

If we look at a brief history of childhood and attitudes to childhood in Western Europe, beginning in the *Middle Ages* (*c*.1000–1453 CE) it is possible to find evidence that children were treated as being 'miniature adults'. They wore the same clothes, ate and drank the same things as adults, were expected to work and were regarded as having the same cognitive abilities as adults. However, this is not to suggest that children at this time were not still as cherished, wanted and loved as at any time in history. What is being explored here is that as society has changed, so too has its concept of the child and childhood.

The notion that children inhabit a special time – that is, childhood, which is somehow different and distinct from adulthood – began to emerge in the fifteenth century, and with it the idea that children may have different needs to adults. It has also been the case that at different times throughout history as different religious notions dominated society's views, these too have impacted on how children and childhood have been viewed. At times children have been seen as naturally wicked and in need of redemption, but by the *nineteenth century* children had come to be seen as being more naughty than wicked (Foley et al., 2001; Luke, 1989; Mills, 1999).

In terms of contemporary views of childhood, in *twenty-first century* Britain there are a range of concepts relating to what we mean by children and childhood. To some extent we are still operating with a romanticized view of childhood, which began to emerge in the *eighteenth century*, which saw children and childhood as a charmed time of purity and innocence (Foley et al., 2001). We still tend to see children and childhood in this way, seeking to protect children from the loss of innocence that comes with being an adult. However, this model of the child brings with it its own tensions, since most children want to explore the world, experiment and 'find things out for themselves', while the adults around them can seem to manage and limit their experiences and development towards adolescence and young adulthood.

The child in contemporary British society

To a greater extent all the models of children and childhood briefly explored above are as seen from an adult point of view. We examined in the previous chapter the notion of how dominant groups can oppress and control those more subordinate to themselves, not necessarily to intentionally cause harm or suffering, but because they believe they know what is best in any given situation. In terms of the adult–child relationship, adults are undeniably in control. This is in part because children are in the process of developing physically, emotionally and cognitively and, obviously, while still very young need a lot of attention, care and support to enable them to simply survive. For these reasons children are also very vulnerable and dependent on those around them who do have the capacity to provide for their needs, and it is in trying to define what the features of this relationship, between the developing and mature human being should be that the different models of the child and childhood proliferate and who holds the power to make their writ run is decided. It is possible to consider the child as being different from adults in that as *biological* entities they are different from adults. However, adults have invented and reinvented the idea of child and childhood as a social construct, to suit our own purposes and depending on the dominant discourse of the time (Cannella, 2002; Robinson, 2005).

We can discuss children as being distinct from adults in biological terms, since children are developing to a physical, emotional and cognitive maturity and because of that are vulnerable in ways adults are not, but we have translated this initial dependence into the industry of childhood, where, in the most extreme cases, children are kept infantilized and not required to have a view, an opinion or a direct input into what might be happening around them and to them, since 'in an important sense the child is an adult in waiting and therefore not part of the social world that counts' (Wyness, 1999: 24).

The concept of childhood

It is when we begin to consider these beliefs about the charmed, pure and innocent nature of the child and how they impact on what we believe children should and should not be exposed to, or encouraged to engage with, that we begin to shape our ideas about childhood. Wyness (1999) in discussing the work of Aries states how 'Aries was concerned with the historical shift in sentiments which shaped a set of ideas and values that gradually crystallized into the idea of the modern child' (Wyness, 1999: 22) and childhood being the space that the child is allowed to be a child in. There can be a tendency to believe that childhood too is a given and that childhood is experienced in a similar way by all young human beings and happens for all children in a similar way. Different families and societies, depending on tradition and cultural practices and, to a very great extent, the economic situation of any given family, will treat childhood in very different ways and have very different expectations for that child.

As we have seen, because childhood is to a greater extent, particularly in industrialized Western nations, a social construct (Barber, 2007: 82; Cannella, 2002) it can be and is defined in different ways by different societies, and for this reason

Activity

What, for you, are the defining features of childhood – how is childhood different and 'special' as compared to adulthood? What happens in childhood that is special to that time and ceases to happen as we become adults?

Now separate your ideas into the following categories:

- what children, as young human beings, actually need to thrive and grow into healthy adults;
- what society also encourages us to provide for children, believing that these are also necessary to enable children to thrive; and
- what society suggests children should not be exposed to as this will harm their development in some way.

Reflecting on this activity, what does this tell you about your model of the child and childhood?

Where did you get these concepts from?

Is there anything you would change in your thinking?

childhood is not experienced in a universal way, across the world. Any one child's experience of childhood will be determined by the society it grows up in and, in the same way, the society will determine how it views the child and what it will seek to provide for the child and expect from it. We have already seen how the notion of what a child is and what childhood might be is determined by prevailing cultural notions. However, one of the problems that this social construction of the notion of children and of childhood leads to is that we lose any sense of benchmarks that might guide us in knowing what it is best to do for children and what children themselves need from their childhoods.

In British society it is generally the norm that children are dealt with differently as compared to adults and often in a more marginal way. It is the adults who have a voice – they make decisions, they control the real power, in terms of money, the media and politics. This is not to say that children are not central to the economic and cultural identity of the adults around them; we can see this in the industry of childcare, education, toy-making and media provision that has developed, dependent entirely on children. Whether it meets the needs of the child we can debate, but what theses industries do achieve is the generation of adult employment and considerable economic wealth. For these reasons, there is a very strong economic argument for the version of childhood currently predominant in society to be perpetuated. However, the downside of this situation is that, again, it is the adults making decisions about what they believe children want from these industries. Even where there are claims that children are consulted with regard to developing toys and media products, these industries are still financed and run by adults (Cannella, 2002). This is not to marginalize caring for and wanting to provide for a loved one in all sorts of ways, because we want to be part of these people's lives and we are concerned for their well-being. Rather, what we are considering is what the actual needs of young human beings are against what we have come to believe they are, and the tensions between these two notions.

The voice of the child

In exploring the concept of child and childhood we have been doing so very much from the stance of being adults, deciding what ought to be the case for children. What we have been denying is that children are beings of themselves and for this reason have what Wyness (1999) describes as an 'ontology'. That is, because something 'is', it commands an authority to be considered and listened to, for its concerns to be canvassed and for its interests and needs – as it considers them to be – to be met. This notion of the ontology of children is what we might now call their 'rights'. Namely the very fact that human beings, and in this instance children, 'are' affords them the expectation of certain responses from those around them.

It is important to consider here the ontology of the child as it impacts on our model of the child and childhood, since a child is not a possession or an object; it is a human being of itself and therefore needs to be accepted on these terms and its wants, needs and desires considered – as are those of adults. This is an important concept to think through. Very often parents will use phrases such as 'this is my child and I decide what is best for it', which seems in the way it is expressed to be to do with ownership of a sort of material good. It often follows from this that parents will then go on to say that because the child is 'theirs' they can, therefore, 'bring it up' and treat them as they see fit. While parents, for many excellent reasons, are often the most-well placed people to bring up their own children, not least because most parents will do so selflessly, providing the best care, love and consideration for the child that they can, the child, from even before it is born, is a member of the wider community and the wider community has a role in bringing up the child. Children are present as beings in society, yet because they lack power (they do not have voting rights, for example) and they have no direct economic earning power (although through their parents they do have buying power) they are generally ignored in the wider social context. To a greater extent children are treated as being invisible – and they remain so, as beings, until the family has undertaken its role to socialize the child into adulthood. Only then will the person have an ontology and become a person with a voice that will be listened too.

The demonization of the child

Adults' attitudes to children are further complicated by the tension between conflicting views held about children, depending on the age of the child. While it is simply easier to romanticize the view of the young child being innocent and charming, even when they might also be actively rejecting this view of themselves by 'being naughty', it is much harder to continue to view children in this way as they become older, more independent and start to want to be young adults. Society has invested hugely in the charming, pure and innocent model of the child. We know that children do grow up and, indeed, must because we need them to take on the role of adult and eventually take over the adult world from us, but we are very unsure of how to actually support the child through the process of becoming an adult. Many of us further exacerbate this tension by giving children mixed messages about what we expect from them. We want children to be charming, pure and innocent, but there is a dominant discourse that also encourages us to think it is amusing to dress children as mini-adults and see them ape the behaviour of adults, although only when we allow it. Children who take licence to 'ape' adult behaviour and actually begin to behave like adults, in earnest, we are very uncertain about dealing with; indeed such children are reported by the media as being 'demon' children.

The dominant discourse of the demon child is one that began to gain its current momentum in the media in the early 1990s, although the notion that children, particularly those on the verge of adulthood, are particularly susceptible to behaving in demonic ways is an idea that has been prevalent since the 1840s, when the term 'juvenile delinquent' was first coined. There is also evidence of concern about adolescents, particularly young men, behaving delinquently, or demonically in reports about wild behaviour of gangs of apprentices, dating from the 1500s (Muncie, 2004). However, it was the terrible and highly atypical murder of the toddler James Bulger in 1993 by two ten-year-old boys that set the scene for the current concern with the demon child (Muncie, 2004: 3). Muncie states: 'The death of James Bulger triggered widespread moral outrage' (ibid.) the ongoing consequences of which Muncie suggests are threefold:

> First, it initiated a reconsideration of the social construction of 10 year olds as 'demons' rather than as 'innocents'. Second, it coalesced with, and helped to mobilize, adult fear and moral panic about youth in general. Third, it legitimized a series of tough law and order responses to young offenders which came to characterize the following decade. (Muncie, 2004: 3)

Barber (2007) suggests this tension arises because, while we encourage children to pretend to the clothes, behaviours and attitudes of adults, we are aware that they have less 'worldly' experience and, to adult eyes, children seem not always to understand the consequences of certain behaviours in particular contexts. We can provide them with the 'tools' of being an adult and encourage them to try them out at home, but we find it hard to accept the consequences of the children and young people then trying out these ideas in the 'real' world. 'Since young adults are knowledgeable and informed without necessarily being wise' (Barber, 2007: 85). Sometimes we 'have propelled children into places and positions before they are ready' (Wyness, 1999: 24). Rogers suggests that these tensions are compounded by adults' attitude to childhood having distilled into two distinct ideologies, or discourses, these being: 'the discourse of welfare and the discourse of control' (Foley et al., 2001: 30).

Further to this, the relativist nature of local practices in bringing up children can cause concern, particularly where not all families keep their children invisible. The media often seems to delight in presenting young people as being 'out of control'. However, in reality, crimes committed by children fell between 2002 and 2006, but the 'numbers of children criminalised had gone up by just over a quarter' (BBC, 2008). In Britain a child can be charged with some crimes at the age of 10, which is also in sharp contrast to other European countries that have a higher age of criminal responsibility and lock up far fewer of their children. Indeed, children in Britain are far more likely to be the victims of crime than to perpetrate them (Narey, 2007). What we do know from research is that where children live in poverty – with its attendant risk factors, of 'poor housing, poor health, educational underachievement, truancy and exclusion' – children and young people in these situations are also at more risk of becoming involved in crime (Narey, 2007). And as Martin Narey, Barnado's chief executive says:

> We can either support [these children] to grow into responsible citizens and valued members of the community or we can reinforce their disadvantage by ridiculing them in the media, expelling them from school and locking them up – pushing them further to the margins, when they most need our help. (Narey, 2007)

Activity

We have discussed how the media is very powerful in supporting and possibly even in establishing dominant discourses. Over the course of a day, note how different media report on the behaviours and actions of older children or adolescents.

Compare the reports in national newspapers and on national news channels with those on local news programmes and in local papers. Often local reporting conveys a better balance between the problems caused by a minority of adolescents and the celebration of the achievements and successes of local young people.

The child's experience

While the 'demon' child is a current dominant discourse, and one that does not stand up to rigorous scrutiny, what we do know about children is that, particularly in educational terms, they 'are achieving better than ever before – gaining good exam results, continuing to university, driving growth in higher skills sectors of the economy' (Narey, 2007).

Let us explore further behind the media spin and examine what children's actual experiences of childhood are. A further dominant discourse with regard to childhood is that children are 'better off' in material terms than they were a few generations ago (Foley et al., 2001: 18). While for many families levels of economic wealth have improved over the past 20 years, there is also evidence that there has been an increase in child poverty. This is further explored in Chapter 8. Although there has been material change, it has been different for different social groups (ibid.). However, all children come under the same pressure to have the same, possibly higher than previously, material expectations and 'change of this nature has led to a stereotyped picture of modern children as spoilt and over-materialistic' (Canella, 2002; Foley et al., 2001: 19). But, again, in this area of their lives, children can be seen to be modelling adult behaviour, since adults too use material goods to 'define their sense of identity', therefore 'we can hardly blame children for doing the same' (Foley et al., 2001: 19). We have allowed the advertising and media industry to pressure us as adults to 'buy' not only for ourselves, but also for children too.

Another common assumption about the change in childhood experience is that children today are healthier than children in the past, and although infant mortality rates fell by 65 per cent between 1963 and 1993, these improvements have only been for certain sectors of society. There is also evidence that suggests the rates of childhood asthma have increased, and that there has been a general deterioration in health and diet (Foley et al., 2001: 20). 'Children in the UK spend most of their waking hours in formal education ... compulsory education is the defining characteristic of modern childhood' (ibid.) and while there is evidence to show that children are attaining higher standards in the subjects they study at school, there is also evidence to show that the improvement in standards have reduced the opportunity for children's personal, social and creative abilities, plus their access to 'free-time' and the chance for unsupervised play. Although there is evidence that children are attaining higher levels in English, mathematics and science at school, this rise in achievement is not true for all groups of children; boys may be becoming increasingly alienated from formal education and 'there is evidence of persistent underachievement by children from some minority ethnic groups, gypsy and traveller children and children who are in care' (DfES 2003a; Foley et al., 2001: 21).

Research has also shown that parents are anxious about allowing children to freely roam without adult supervision and that there is concern about a rise in violent crimes against children, although it is less clear if these incidents have risen or it is the fear of them that has led to a change in parenting behaviour (Foley et al., 2001: 22). Compounding the concerns about children being able to play without adult supervision is the rise in the home as a place of leisure and entertainment, where most households have at least one television, video player and DVD player. Many households also have computers and access to the Internet. Not only do children have access to these forms of entertainment, but much of it is aimed directly at them, and while there is also concern that too much access to television and games consoles exacerbates anti-social behaviour, research shows that children are also quite able to reject media messages they do not like and are not 'at the mercy' of the media, passively soaking up everything they watch, as is sometimes suggested (ibid.).

Children's lives and experiences need to be placed in the wider social context in which we all live. Children and adults face, and deal with, a wide diversity of experiences. What must be considered is the control children have over their own lives and experiences.

Case study

James, known as Jimmy, was a 12-year-old boy in a Year 6 class in a North-West London primary school. He was an Irish, gypsy traveller whose family had recently moved from their trailer on the local authority travellers' site into settled accommodation.

Jimmy was the eldest of seven children, having five brothers and a very recent baby sister. Four of the boys were at school and the entire family was delighted the new baby was a girl, which was evident from the stories the boys told about their baby sister and how they would also write about her and want to take things home from school to show her.

Jimmy's dad, also called James, had recently, through the death of his own father, become the 'head' of the entire extended family in the local area. By default Jimmy then became 'head' of the family at school, being responsible not only for his brothers, but a number of cousins too.

This was Jimmy's second year at school, and the decision had been made to place him in a school year lower than his chronological age. He was physically bigger than the other children in his class and emotionally more mature; he was well liked by the other children but received a mixed response from teachers. He was very good at attending, rarely wore uniform to school, hardly ever badly behaved, was very funny and quick witted and, it also transpired, could drive.

Jimmy had a number of cousins at the school, two of whom caused the staff a lot of problems, their behaviour was very disruptive, sometimes violent, and the eldest boy's attendance was erratic since he often went to work with his father. This frustrated and pleased his teacher, since she was pleased he was absent and she did not have to deal with his behaviour, but it also interrupted the progress he was making. It further frustrated some staff that the cousin would do what Jimmy said, but would not obey them. Sometimes, they felt their authority and values particularly challenged when they were forced to seek Jimmy's help to manage his cousin. From Jimmy's point of view, this was a normal way to do things and he was often very embarrassed and apologetic that he could not control his cousin better and that the cousin was letting the family down so badly.

Jimmy's Year 6 teacher was very committed to working with traveller families in a supportive and proactive way, and in working with the Traveller Support Service from the local authority. To the teacher it was clear that in many ways Jimmy had 'out-grown' primary school, the very real responsibilities he was used to dealing with and the authority he was used to commanding with adults outside school caused tensions in the school. However, it was usually Jimmy who realized that power was organized differently in the school and generally he was

continued

continued

prepared to defer to the teachers. He was also bright enough to see the irony in that at one moment he was being treated like a child and in the next his help was wanted to deal with his cousin, and even to manage his aunt and uncle when they were aggressive towards the school.

Over the course of Year 6 Jimmy learnt to read and write. His parents were very pleased – for a number of reasons. His mother had come from a settled background and felt school to be important; for his father it was both expedient (particularly when having to deal with the settled community) and added to the respect he and Jimmy had in their own community. That Jimmy took his reading book home was an opportunity not lost on the teachers' of his brothers and cousins. If Jimmy took his book home – didn't they think they should too? However, Jimmy's mum often said having to listen to four boys reading was a mixed blessing.

Jimmy himself had put a lot of effort into this task, partly because being able to master these skills added to his authority and standing in the family, but also because he knew that it meant he would probably be allowed, by his parents, not to have to go to secondary school. Again Jimmy was quite astute enough to know the uneasy alliance he had struck with the authorities in his primary school he was unlikely to achieve at secondary. He also knew, from older members of his own family, that he would get a far rougher ride from the older children at secondary school. By the end of Year 6 Jimmy felt school had done as much for him as it could and that he too had done his bit for the school. However he had also come to the considered opinion that it was time to go and take up his place as a man in his community and help his dad in the more important tasks of managing and looking after his community.

Listening to children

Two of the most influential changes in terms of consulting with children and listening to their voice are:

- the United Kingdom's ratification of the United Nations Convention on the Rights of the Child (UNCRC) in 1991; and
- the Children's Act 2004.

In ratifying the UNCRC the British government has agreed to honour the rights set out in the convention, 'except in those areas where the government has entered a specific reservation' (Directgov, 2008). Since the treaty came into force in 1992, children in Britain have been entitled to over 40 specific rights, including having the 'right to have their views respected, and to have their best interests considered at all times' (Directgov, 2008). However, a convention is not the same as *law*, and the British government is not legally bound to adhere to the convention. In the same way, children can 'not bring a case to court if they believe that one or more of their Convention rights are being infringed'

(NSPCC, 2008a). Indeed the British government has been criticized by the UN Committee on the Rights of the Child, to whom it reports every year, for its failure to make progress in securing aspects of the articles it ratified. However, through the Children's Act 2004 the government has responded to some of the criticisms of the Committee and has also enshrined in British law the requirement that in separation or divorce proceedings that come before a court, the wishes of any children affected must be 'the court's paramount consideration in any decision relating to his or her upbringing' (DCSF, 2007c: 42). It is also from the Children's Act 2004 that we have the five outcomes of the ECM agenda, and the requirement for all agencies who work to support children and their families to work together and to work with children and families, listening to their voices in determining how provision should be 'rolled-out'.

One of the most important messages that the ratification of the UNCRC and the subsequent legislation that has been briefly outlined above signals, is that, by acknowledging children have rights, it gives them an ontology – it acknowledges, partly in law, that they are beings 'of themselves' and therefore can speak directly for themselves and are not at risk of having their wishes reinterpreted or misinterpreted through the channel of the adults around them. The notion of the child's voice is further discussed in Chapter 7.

Different agencies – different models of the child

Since the seventeenth- and eighteenth-century, philosophers and those interested in exploring what it is to be a child and that childhood might be different from adulthood, and how childhood might determine the adult the child will become, have tended to pursue the argument through two approaches. The first of these theoretical approaches stresses the role of a child's innate nature in determining the person they will be, including the part developmental psychology has to play in the nature of the child. The second approach stresses the role of the environment in which the child grows up in as the determining factor – that is, how they are nurtured.

Nature

In terms of the 'nature' side of the debate, some of the most influential work has been that of Jean Piaget, who formulated his theory of cognitive, or 'thinking abilities' development in the 1950s. Piaget is known as a cognitive developmental theorist and viewed biology – the genetic make-up of the child – as being the most important distinguishing effect on how a child will develop. Through working with children and observing how they solved problems he set them, Piaget theorized that childrens' thinking and thought processes are very different to those of an adult. He proposed that the combination of the environment a child grows up in and the experiences that the environment provides a child, coupled with the natural stages of cognitive development a child passes through to adulthood, will impact on the cognitive development of the child. His theory develops the notion that children learn by exploring their environment and essentially 'testing how things work'. Through these experiences they build up schemas of understanding about the world which, as they learn new things, they adapt to assimilate the new information. His work has been very influential in establishing the notion that children are 'different' from adults, not just biologically, but that they think in different ways too and need an environment that allows them to play, test and explore the world around them.

Piaget's four main stages of cognitive development are summarized below.

Stage 1 Sensorimotor thought (birth to 2 years)
In this stage thinking is in terms of responding to and possibly interpreting inputs from the senses. In this stage children cannot think in an abstract way, that is, hypothesize, or think about things that do not have a direct bearing on their senses at that point. If their primary care provider is absent and they want contact with them, they will respond to that desire, rather than be able to reason that he or she is elsewhere and will come back soon. By about 15 months children begin to become more exploratory and to make causal links between events and their actions. For example, a random action that results in an event that interests and pleases the child will be made deliberately and intentionally in the future. Pressing a button on a washing machine or toy will cause something to happen.

Stage 2 Pre-operational thought (2–7 years)
Children begin to acquire language and develop the capacity to hold mental images and remember things, although they cannot think logically and deal with more than one idea at a time. For example, a child who is in the pre-operational stage will not be able to answer a question like: 'I have a handful of sweets, 2 sweets are red and 3 sweets are green. What do I have more of, the number of sweets altogether or green sweets?'

Stage 3 Concrete operational thought (7–11 years)
This is a significant stage of development for children as it is at this point that they begin to be able to see the world, ideas and actions from the point of view of others. This is know as being able to decentre.

Stage 4 Formal operational thought (age 11 to adulthood)
It is in this stage that children become able to think hypothetically and outside their direct experience, for example, to imagine worlds, as in fantasy stories which do not exist in real experience; similarly, they are able to engage in abstract thinking such as is needed in mathematics.

One of the most significant things about this notion of child development is that the child must pass through each stage, and in the order as described by Piaget. It is important – and a developmental necessity in terms of the overall cognitive maturation of the child – that they 'complete' each aspect of cognitive development and understanding before they can move on to the next stage (Bentham, 2004). While it is unarguably the case that children change physically in their development from babies to adulthood, Piaget's notion of cognitive stages raises as many issues as it seems to explain. Other child development theorists have significantly challenged the work of Piaget, for example, the child psychologist Margaret Donaldson (Donaldson, 1984). While Piaget's work is useful in that it provides a framework, an overview, of how children's cognitive abilities might develop, it is criticized as being too rigid in tying development stages to chronological age and adhering to the notion that each stage has to be passed through before the child is able to master the cognitive challenges of the next stage.

Other theories that have impacted on and influenced our knowledge, understanding and beliefs about child development, and therefore our models of the child, are theories with regard to learning development. One of the most influential theorists in this area is B.F. Skinner (1905–90). Skinner was a leading 'behaviourist', behaviourism being a theory that focuses on behaviour as the objective of all human functioning. Human beings are motivated to behave in certain ways depending on the sense of innate or extrinsic reward they feel as a result of that action. These ideas are the basis of many reward/sanction-based discipline systems used with children in formal education settings. Children are rewarded, through praise or in other ways, to encourage them to behave in ways that are wanted. Conversely, sanctions are applied when children exhibit unwanted behaviours, to discourage such behaviour. However, critics of this method of managing children see this approach as being akin to coercion, or brainwashing, or that children only learn to do things if there is a reward attached and they will not learn to manage their own behaviour in the absence of an incentive.

John Bowlby (1969–80), is acknowledged as one of the most prominent theorists to begin to research social effects on development, in particular he is famous for his 'attachment theory' (Flanagan, 1999). When Bowlby first began discussing this theory his work centred on the importance, in developmental terms, of the attachment a child forms with its mother. However, the notion that a child can form the necessary nurturing attachment, needed for healthy social and psychological development, only with its mother has been developed by other theorists working in this area. The current accepted theory is that children can form a number of attachments with adults other than the biological mother, what is important is that children need caring and nurturing relationships in order to thrive, and not simply that basic needs for food and shelter are met (Foley et al., 2001: 211). This theme is picked up in the next chapter, in examining what children need from families.

A further influential theorist in the area of child development is Erikson who in the 1960s, devised a model of human social development that focuses more on the impact of background and environment on development, rather than genetic determiners. This is known as a psychosocial model (Miller, 2003). The importance of this theory of development is that it seeks to explore how the beliefs, attitudes and values we grow up to hold are shaped by our genetic pre-disposition towards stimuli and how the environment we grow up in impacts on those innate characteristics. Therefore, Erikson maintains, we are distinctly shaped by our formative experiences. If this is so, then the experiences a child will have while in an Early Years setting or in school will have a considerable long-term effect on the adult that child becomes, including on the attitudes, beliefs and values they will hold.

The models we have briefly looked at here are very much associated with educational model of the child. Those who are primarily concerned with a child in terms of their health may be focused on different signifiers of development. For example, there is already a range of ante-natal screening that takes place while the child is still in the womb, to determine if the child has any 'health problems' prior to birth. Parents, too, are given plenty of health advice about how to ensure the child is born into an healthy environment, that it is provided with the right nourishment and that its physical health and growth are monitored against 'normal' trajectories of healthy development. In part this is because we know that health during childhood will impact on the health of the adult and that a child that is healthy is more likely to thrive in all aspects of their life. This concern for monitoring children's healthy development is expressed by the Institute of Medicine Staff in the following way: 'the nation must have an improved understanding of the factors that affect health and effective strategies for measuring and using information on children's health' (Institute of Medicine Staff, 2004: 14). In exploring the notion of the model of the healthy child, Warsh writes of the growth of the 'health movement' that filled homes with 'the technology of personal hygiene (washbasins, toilets, toothbrushes, soap, and tissues) and then made sure that these products were used. It was the job for a new kind of expert: a professional health educator' (Warsh, 2005: 24). Warsh (2005) goes on to describe the three principles on which this movement was based: that no matter how meagre a families resources everyone could maintain their own good health through 'preventive health care based on good habits of eating, sleeping, and keeping clean' (Warsh, 2005: 25).

There is no doubt that monitoring children's health over the past few decades has greatly improved the overall well-being of children, and this has included 'reducing mortality and morbidity from many infectious diseases and accidental causes, increasing access to health care, and reducing environmental contaminants' (Institute of Medicine Staff, 2004: 14). However, just as there are criticisms of the various cognitive developmental models educationalists use of children, so too the health sector has critics of its models, the significant issue of working with a 'model' being that the model presupposes that anything that does not fit the model is 'deviant'. Again, the child, that is, the person – the ontology of the child – can get lost in trying to fix the child to meet the model or in discarding the child that cannot be fixed. We have seen this happening in the past where children with disabilities and learning difficulties that cannot be 'fixed' are placed out of the way of mainstream society and their families left unsupported and marginalized.

In a multi-agency approach to working with children, there is the potential to have a range of different agents' models of what constitutes a child – and therefore the best way of dealing with the child may cause tensions between professionals. So far we have only considered the models used by educationalist or health-care workers. There are also the social care model of the child and the youth criminal justice model to take into account – to a greater extent the social care model of the child is explored in the following chapter of this book. Those who have central to their working lives the concern for the welfare of the whole child, have a duty to resolve any differences in approaches in working with children through agencies by talking to each other but, most crucially, by talking to and listening to the child.

Activity

Your model of the child and childhood
Think through the experience you have in working with children. Which of the models briefly outlined above seem to agree most with your ideas and experience?

What evidence do you have to defend your ideas? Can you talk about instances of working with children when they have behaved in the way described by your preferred theorist?

How has the model presented by your chosen theorist helped you provide better for the needs of children?

Of the other theories, what is it that you do not agree with? What evidence do you have to support your position?

This chapter has explored the concept of the child, and what childhood might be, through notions, or dominant discourses, that currently have a strong influence on how these concepts are viewed in society. More significantly, it is not only how these discourses explain children and childhood that we need to consider, but the impact these ideas have on public policy. The prevailing concept of what it is a child might be influences all practice that relates to children, from the way children will be treated in their own homes, to what happens to them in the Early Years setting and at school. These notions affect how children will be treated by health-care workers, child protection workers and how they will be dealt with by the Youth Justice System and the media. It is a symbiotic relationship, the dominant discourses feed public opinion and policy and vice versa.

The individuals in any group in society are linked to one to another by the means through which they communicate. A universally predominant way of communicating is through spoken and, often, written language, that is, through discourse. The 'centrality of language in social life' (Matheson, 2005: 2) serves a range of purposes: not only can we pass on information to each other, but the very language – choice of words – we choose to use to pass on information will shape the attitudes beliefs and values of the group, that is we 'cannot separate out people's thoughts and actions from the communicative means that they use to perform them' (Matheson, 2005: 3), what we say and write is what we do (Mills, 1997: 5).

> Discourse must be understood in its widest sense: every utterance assuming a speaker and a hearer, and in the speaker, the intention of influencing the other in some way ... It is every variety of oral discourse of every nature from trivial conversation to the most elaborate oration ... .(Mills, 1997: 5)

As has been explored in Chapter 1, the language of those groups that have the power in any given situation can be used, overtly or inadvertently, to disadvantage subordinate groups. In some instances the discourse of certain groups becomes a dominant discourse and is treated as if it is the belief of a wide audience, sometimes of a society itself, that is, 'certain representations of the social world' come to be predominant or accepted view of how things should be (Matheson, 2005: 1). In Britain, a society that has a well-established, very complex, media industry (ibid.), many ideas can be circulated in the public arena, and where certain notions are 'picked-up' by media that command a large audience, then the way in which they express ideas can establish what can go on to become a dominant discourse.

Some of the dominant discourses as they relate to children and childhood have been explored in some detail above, both those perpetuated by the media and those used by different professionals concerned with children's education, health or social care. We have also already touched on two further discourses, that of a discourse of welfare set against a discourse of control. These are important ideas to consider, particularly for those who work with children and write policy for children. That is, is social policy and legislation there to protect the welfare of children, or to control them? Under ECM, there may be further tensions here, where those agencies from a child protection and health backgrounds may have different notions of what is in the best interests of the child – the welfare of the child – while schools, education and the criminal justice system can be seen to derive from a tradition of the discourse of control.

It is not by accident that a central tenet of the ECM agenda is that of well-being. We know that many children, through poverty and other impoverishing experiences, do not experience well-being or have the means to achieving it in the future for themselves. Therefore, we need to be concerned, not only for the material aspect of children's lives, but also the wider aspects of how they experience their lives socially and emotionally. Traditional attitudes to children have not stopped abuse of adult power over children, whether intentional or unwitting; however, changing practice to ensure children's ideas and wishes are routinely considered is a model of working with children that will be very challenging for some practitioners, teachers and others.

One way of beginning to resolve these tensions is to discuss issues with the children themselves, 'Since Children themselves might have something particular to say about their own world and to contribute to decision-making in relation to this environment' (Foley et al., 2001: 82). The notion of children's voice is explored further in Chapter 7. But if we consider where the power has traditionally been when it comes to judgements about children, whether from a welfare or control perspective, it has not been with the child. This has changed somewhat with the Children's Act and the notion of Children's Voice however, if we consider where we are at present: 'What do all these stories tell us? First, they regularly present children's vulnerability. Second, they confirm adults' assertion of fundamental rights over young bodies and minds. Third, they demonstrate the diversity of children and their varying susceptibility to the control of the powerful' (Warsh, 2005: 15).

Further reading

'Say it your own way': Children's participation in assessment (that is, in consulting children to help practitioners and others make assessment about children's needs): www.barnardos.org.uk/sayityourownway

The full list of articles that comprises the UN Convention of the Rights of the Child can be accessed at: www.everychildmatters.gov.uk/_files/589DD6D3A29C929ACB148DB3F13B01E7 .pdf

Useful websites

www.dcsf.gov.uk/

www.cyh.com

www.bbc.co.uk/children/

www.surestart.gov.uk/surestartservices/childcare/childrensinformationservice/

www.familyinformationservices.org.uk/

3

Families

This chapter explores:

- what is meant by the term 'family';
- the child in the family;
- what Early Years settings and schools need to consider when working with children and their families; and
- Children's Centres as models of good practice.

In Chapter 2, in exploring different models of the child and what might constitute childhood, one of the ideas examined was the notion that childhood is a time when children, as young and developing human beings, are vulnerable, particularly physically and emotionally. In Chapter 1 we also explored that, in order to flourish, human beings – and, in this instance, children – need to have access to certain goods, advantages and benefits to thrive and achieve well-being. For many reasons, some of which are explored in this chapter, it is usually what we commonly term 'the family' that is best placed to provide the conditions for a child to flourish, indeed the current government's Children's Plan states: 'families are the bedrock of society and the place for nurturing happy, capable and resilient children' (DCSF, 2007d).

However, the notion of what might constitute a family, or family unit, is a greatly contested issue both in the media and in public policy, as is the best practice a family should adopt towards bringing up any children within the family unit. This chapter explores some of the dominant discourses that relate to what families should look like and how they should behave, and it raises issues about how Early Years settings and schools can engage with families to best support them and meet the requirements of the ECM agenda.

Why the family is so useful

In real terms the notion of 'family' 'has no fixed meaning and takes on meaning as an object of knowledge within discourses, it is unstable and continuously being reshaped within particular historical contexts' (Chambers, 2001: 26). There is a very powerful dominant discourse that harks back to a golden time of 'the family', the notion of parents and children, and possibly grandparents too, living side by side in domestic bliss, with 'dad' going out to work as the breadwinner and 'mum' supervising the children and generally keeping things shipshape at home. However, even the most cursory research into the notion of family will quickly show that families and family life is messy, and very often noisy; it is about facing challenges and celebrating successes; it is an experience of great highs and equally desperate lows – and it has always been like this.

In order to survive all societies 'establish institutions that will rear and educate the young. In the majority of societies the main institution for this is the family' (Wyse and Hawtin, 2000: 86) and as part of living in a family we 'pick up' skills, knowledge and understanding about how to survive as a human being. Not only in the pragmatic sense of the actual skills, knowledge and understanding we need to live, but also the skills, knowledge and understanding we need to thrive and function in the society into which we are born. For these reasons our social understandings and behaviours will usually reflect the ideas and notions of the people around us whom we grew up with and, since most families operate in a wider social structure, the family's beliefs, attitudes and values will often reflect their immediate society.

For these reasons the notion of family serves two very useful societal functions: (1) it will rear any children born into the family in terms of providing food and shelter and, in the case of most families do so with a lot of love and cherishing, and (2) it will teach the child how to function as a valuable member of the society it is born into since the 'typical mechanism of transmission, both horizontally and vertically, is through imitation' (Combrinck-Graham, 2006: 97) and the child will grow up imitating those around it. This, can however, be a cause for concern if those the child is imitating behave in ways that lie outside the dominant discourse of 'acceptable behaviour'; so it also follows that where we might want to change or influence a child's behaviour we have to work with the whole family, not just the child, to effect those changes. Settings and schools therefore that do not work with the family will find it particularly demanding to modify the attitudes and behaviours of challenging children, unless they are prepared to work closely with the family too. Indeed, it may be the case that to change family behaviours it is necessary to work with more than one generation of that family.

Given that the family is a powerful force for socialization, those who control the notion of what family is also control what goes on in families and what is 'passed' on as normative behaviour. We have already explored how public policy is shaped by dominant discourses espoused by the media, social commentators, educationalists, politicians and those who work in health care, and how those in control, who drive the dominant discourses, can use them to oppress those who are more marginalized. In this way, there abound in society notions of what families 'should' be and much time is taken up and harm done by trying to 'fix' those families that do not fit the model of the dominant discourse.

What do we mean by 'family'?

Activity

Who is 'our family'?
You are organizing a big party to celebrate an important event in your life. You want the people who mean most to you to be there. Write a list of names of the people you want to invite.

Looking at your list, how many of the people on the list would you consider are actually related to you by birth?
How many of the people on the list are there because you consider them related to you through your partner?
Who on the list is not 'related' to you at all, but has been an important part of your life – perhaps since you were a child?
Who on your list is there because they are close friends?
How has the list changed from who you might have included on your list 10 years ago?
Are there people on the list you would prefer not to invite, but feel 'I have to'? If you actually cross them off your list, how does it look now?
Are there people on the list who, in you day-to-day life, you rely on more than those you are related to?
What does this say about who in our lives are important and who we might class as 'family'?

The now idealized notion of the 'nuclear' family harks back to the post-war West trying to rebuild itself after the second devastating war in the space of 50 years. Post-1945 government money was targeted at house-building, education and welfare policies, which enabled families to thrive on one income and in a strongly supportive government welfare society (Chambers, 2001; Robinson, 2005; Walsh, 2006: 29). As the West has recovered from the ravages of the first half of the twentieth century and families and individuals have become wealthier, in a buoyant, peaceful economic climate, the nature of what the family needs to be, both for children, individuals and the state has changed. We now live in a world that can support both economically and socially an increasingly diverse society, and this impacts not only on diversity in family 'units' but in wider terms too – in the range of cultures a society can accommodate, and ways life can be lived.

It has already been suggested that the family unit serves two important functions: first, to provide the necessary nurturing a child needs to survive, thrive and enjoy well-being and, secondly, families usually serve to pass on to the child the culture the child is born into, and for this reason the child might be seen not only as an end in themselves, but also as the future of the society in which it grows up. The initial nurture provided by the child's immediate family is widened and extended as the child grows up and moves into other areas of care and education.

There is a strong historical and political tradition in British culture that seems to suggest the best and most usual – or 'normal' – family is that where children are nurtured by their own biological parents, who are a married heterosexual couple. Such a 'family' may be a politically useful economic unit, but it does not necessarily reflect the family experience of many, or even most, children and may put artificially high demands on individuals to try and meet an unrealistic ideal. This 'norm' of family life, or the nuclear family, is as we have just seen a quite recent and fictitious notion, but over a short time it has become the case that any family that does not fit this norm is seen as being a problem, not only to itself but for wider society too. The knock-on effect of this that the media and public policy rewards those who can or do adhere to the nuclear family ideal and, at best, tries to makes those that do not, conform or, at worst, uses them as scapegoats for the perceived problems in society.

> During the 1980s, the British Conservative government promoted the myth of a fixed and unchanging nuclear familial type as essentially white Anglo-Saxon Protestant. This version of the family was represented as biologically and psychically natural, stable and universal, and yet also as vulnerable, in a state of crisis and under threat. (Chambers, 2001: 16)

However, exploration of the realities of 'family' life shows that rather than the nuclear family being the norm, research presents a picture of family life which includes 'family units' comprised of one or two parents, parents of different sexes or the same sex and children with siblings who may share one or both parents or be step-siblings. Many families are intergenerational, accommodating grandparents and great-grandparents, or extended family units with aunts, uncles and cousins living in the family home. In some family units one parent may work or both parents may work – or there may be no working parents, but a grandparent or 'grown-up' child may be the working adult. In some family units parents cannot work because they are disabled and it may be that the children perform what are usually regarded as the 'parenting' or caring roles within the unit. It is also the case, again despite what the dominant discourse would have us believe, that this variety in family units is not specific to one aberrant sector of society; family units that do not adhere to the nuclear ideal can thrive across all social classes and all ethnicities.

Having explored the notion of the nuclear family as an ideal of what a family should be, and found it to be an ideal founded on rather flimsy pretexts, this does not detract from the importance of a family unit or household, in terms of their capacity and potential to provide a safe, loving, nurturing environment in which children can thrive. Children need love, care and guidance, and the availability of these advantages and benefits of family life are not special only to nuclear families.

Activity

The nuclear family 'ideal' is usually conceived of as being a family unit comprised of children living in the same household as their biological mother and father – the parents being married to each other and this being their only marriage.

How does this model of family life reflect:

• your own childhood?
• your current, or intended, family situation?
• the family experience of your close friends and siblings?

Of the families you are related to or friends with, how many of them reflect the nuclear family model?

The enduring legacy of the nuclear family ideal

Having explored the notion that the nuclear family is less the norm than has been promulgated, it is still important to examine some of the impacts on the cultural consciousness and public policy that the concept of the nuclear family has had, as these ideals continue to have an enduring impact, particularly in the public domain. Very often Early Years settings and schools continue to behave as if the nuclear family is the family experience of the majority, if not all, of the children and families they work with. That this is so is evident in policy and practice, and can be reflected in the attitudes of the practitioners, teachers and others. It seems as if, in taking up a position in an Early Years setting or school, adults leave what they know to be 'real life' at the door and revert to the dominant discourse of the nuclear family as they enter the setting or school. For example, it is often the mother who is still perceived as being the main carer for a child; most directives from settings and schools are aimed at 'mum', and learning activities featuring play corners, stories and so on often reflect the ideal of the nuclear family, rather than reinforcing a positive image of the family the child may actually experience.

While the nuclear family ideal is currently being challenged, there are aspects of the notion that are deeply entrenched in the dominant cultural and policy approaches to family, and these principles of what a normal family is continue to marginalize many well-functioning family units. Such assumptions implicit in the idealized notion of family not only mitigate against the acceptance of diversity, but they can also be used to draw attention to the families that are not a reflection of the nuclear 'norm', and because they are not normal they are open to the accusation of being deviant.

Activity

Whether wittingly or unwittingly, when we are trying to devise activities to do with children we often find ourselves hard pressed for time and it can be easy to fall back on ideas and materials that, on reflection, we might find are not really as suitable as first thought.

The next time you are in an Early Years setting or school, take some time to look reflectively at how the environment the children are in reflects current dominant discourses.

Some ideas about elements of practice to think about specifically are given below.

• Where there are play corners, home corners or other areas set up to reflect a learning activity, how do the toys and materials in those areas reflect idealized notion of families and adult roles?
• In talking to children and encouraging them to talk and engage in activities, what language are adults using? Look out for statements that reinforce stereotypes about parenting and family life.
• Do the books, both fiction and non-fiction, used with children reflect the children's actual experiences?
• How is material sent home addressed? Who is the expected audience for the information?
• Has your setting or school had any recent in-service training about these issues, or even had a staff meeting to talk through a policy to ensure it is seeking to include all families and embrace the wider diversity of children's family units?

A further erosion of the nuclear family model has been through political changes over the past, at least 30, years that has seen power in families as being more equally shared across family members. The nuclear family model has dad as the main power force, particularly in terms of financial power, and mum as the power in the kitchen. In reality, many families have more complex and varied systems of negotiating and managing financial and domestic power. Not only this, but it is unlikely that whoever holds what responsibilities will remain a constant, as the family dynamics change over time – as children grow up, as family members in the more extended family may need extra input, as jobs change, so family life changes. There is also evidence that shows families are getting smaller, with 1.8 children per family now being the average, the average at which women have their first child has gone up to 28 and many more people seem to be living alone, either through choosing to stay single longer than in the recent past or because of the increased levels in divorce, so couples that have separated are now seeking two homes where previously they had one (Wyse and Hawtin, 2000: 93). Where 18 per cent of homes were one person homes in 1971, this rose to 29 per cent in 2000 and is predicted to be 36 per cent by 2016 (ibid.). Similarly, households comprised of married couples, which was 71 per cent of all households 25 years ago, now constitutes about 50 per cent of households. Further to this it is estimated that by 2034 the number of retired people will constitute 50 per cent of the population, while the number of children will have fallen by 15 per cent. These figures will prompt further rethinking of what society means when it talks of 'family' (Wyse and Hawtin, 2000: 93–4).

There has also been an increase in the number of one-adult, or one-parent households and an increase in the number of children living in homes where the caring adults are not married (Wyse and Hawtin, 2000: 94).

Who should be bringing up the children?

We have already explored how human beings, and in this instance children, need access to certain goods in order to thrive and achieve well-being and the family is often best placed to provide for these needs, not least because of the necessary and strong caring bonds between those in a family. However, we have also examined that families can come in many forms, the central important point being that the child is in a family unit where the goods it needs to thrive are being provided. Children do not need only their biological parents for this to happen, indeed in some instances it is not possible or safe for children to be with one or both biological parents – and there are many adults who are excellent 'parents' in all but biological terms. However, what we have learnt about families is that where a family unit is most successful in ensuring children are thriving, it is where the child does have contact with adults who do take on particular roles. These roles are important as they often serve as role models for the children in the family to learn about how to be adults and then, in their turn, how to raise their family. For example, there is the role of 'father' and 'mother' and while it is not necessary for those that take these roles to be the biological parents of the child in the family – or even for the roles to be specific to gender or for those who are the 'mother' and 'father' to live in the same household – what the child gains from being parented by those in these roles and, in turn, learn about parenting and what it is to be an adult in society, are highly influential in securing a child's well-being.

Historically in Western societies where a relationship between parents breaks down, where there is a mother it is often the case that she, because of some perceived particular bond with the child or children, will continue to be the main caregiver. However, it needs to be considered that this is yet another fictitious societal concept about women looking after the children at home and men remaining in continuous employment to provide for the family. Where women now have the capacity, and desire, to work as well as have children, there is no innate reason why women should automatically have custody rights over children; indeed the marginalization fathers can feel in these situations often exacerbates what is already a crisis situation for any children involved (Chambers, 2001: 23). This, coupled with the need for children to have a range of adult role models in their lives, has increased awareness of the importance of the need for someone to be in the father role for children and, where possible, for fathers to have a role in their children's lives. 'Fathers' involvement in child rearing is an additional route to positive outcomes for children ... children of highly involved fathers score better on measures of intelligence, school achievement, mature social behavior' (Berk, 2004: 9; DfES, 2007c: 6).

Sometimes settings and schools automatically send materials home assuming the mother is the audience for the material. In the case of children whose parents do not live in the same home, there is debate over whether settings and schools have a duty to ensure the 'other' parent also receives the information.

Stating that children need to have a significant adult that fulfils the father role in their lives can be highly contentious. The contention arises because raising the issue can quickly lead to charges of sexism and racism. The charge that the claim is sexist is based in discourses linked to aspects of feminist theory. Some groups will claim that it is a woman's right to choose whether she is in contact with the father of her child or children. Indeed, it may be the case that it is not safe for either the woman or the child(ren) to be in contact with their father and, therefore, to suggest that children 'should' have a father undoes all the hard work achieved in terms of equality for women over the past 30 years. The charge of racism arises because exploring the role of fathers can lead to the dominant discourse that couches discussion about absent fathers in terms of them being 'offenders' and cites the worst offenders of absent fatherhood as being black Caribbean men, and that absent fatherhood is somehow a lifestyle choice of Caribbean men. To state the issue like this bases the reason for being an absent father on the fact the men are black Caribbean in ethnicity, not on the fact that they may be absent for all the reasons that apply to absent white fathers too. Discussing the issue of the importance of fathers for children in these terms polarizes the issue and perpetuates existing systems of oppression. The concern is not with whether women or men should be in charge of who brings up the children or that white men are better fathers than black Caribbean men; the issue is how vulnerable families can be supported to ensure their children have significant adults in their lives who will parent them in an appropriate way.

The research shows that where fathers are involved in their children's lives:

- there is a positive relationship to later educational achievement;
- there is an association with good parent–child relationship in adolescence; and
- children in separated families are more protected from mental health problems. (DfES, 2007c: 6)

Case study

Many Children's Centres lead the way in directly seeking to involve fathers in the lives of their children. Most Children's Centres run fathers' groups; for example, one Children's Centre in Kent regularly holds group meeting on Saturday morning at the Centre. The group is currently run by a male health worker, but has been run by the female manager of the centre. The fathers come together and spend quality time with their children in an informal and supportive setting where not only can they be with their children, but discuss with other fathers the worries, frustrations and anxieties of being a dad.

Without access to groups like this fathers can feel marginalized and excluded from their children's lives. Until recently the dominant discourse has focused on the importance of mothers in a child's life and not provided a vehicle for fathers to know what their role is, or to know who to talk to, even to ask if they are going about it the right way or not – particularly if their own father was not part of their childhood.

The group can take up particular issues to explore and provide links to other support agencies if fathers request them. This might be of help to fathers desperate to provide for their children, to find work, or to return to adult education where they want to further develop their skills.

Guardian journalist Simon Rawles, writing about fathers' groups, says: 'family services are beginning to recognise that they need to adapt to meet fathers' needs' and that it is important 'to make dads feel that their contribution is worthwhile' (Rawles, 2005).

It is also worth noting that it is now required that primary care trusts, local authorities and children's services should provide targeted information and training to fathers.

Bad parents

In Chapter 2 we explore the notion of the dominant discourse of the 'demon' child, perhaps not surprisingly there is also a prevailing concept of the 'bad' parent. The bad parent is usually portrayed as being a negligent parent, possibly through misuse of drugs and/or alcohol, possibly criminal and always depicted as someone who lives like this through choice; they are usually poor, but poor because of their lifestyle choices not through lack of opportunity. This is not to say that there are parents who behave in ways likely to harm their children, but there are also parents who struggle with sometimes overwhelming challenges to parent their children, yet are still labelled as bad parents. 'For a small minority of parents who have lost, or never had, the capacity to parent responsibly, public services must be ready to intervene promptly and sensitively' (DfES, 2007c: 7).

In the dominant discourses relating to families there has been particular focus on what is termed 'family breakdown' and in particular how the breakdown of the family results in bad parenting and directly contributes to a decline in moral standards and a generation of children who are out of control (Thompson, 1998). The use of the family breakdown concept has enabled policy-makers who wish to explain challenges in society and, in particular mask issues such as poverty by 'shifting the blame onto parents (particularly mothers) who fail to conform to the nuclear model' (Chambers, 2001: 19) and can be labelled 'bad parents', by claiming that any perceived problems in society are as a result of bad parents, particularly those who cannot hold a family together, to focus attention away from factors such as inequalities, poverty, poor housing and lack of opportunity that might be causing the problems but are also harder to address.

Rather than focus on how some 'family' groups do not seem to fit the 'norm', and should be somehow 'fixed' by intervention, it is more helpful to explore what are the strengths of any given family unit, particularly in supporting the child or children, and to work with that. This is what Chambers refers to as 'the "strength resiliency" perspective' (Chambers, 2001: 13). That is to say, what is important in a family is the strengths it does have and how those can be used to find and use strategies to enable a child to thrive, rather than focusing on what the family does not have. For example, while families may have 'one parent' many one-parent families are successful because there is a network of friends and family that can support the family. The focus therefore, should not be on how the family is vulnerable because there is only one parent, but on how the support networks that are in place can be best used, supported and strengthened. The importance of the notion of resilience, and what resilience is, is explored in greater depth in Chapter 8.

In popular cultural mythology, there is also nothing worse than a bad mother. And there is no worse label for a woman than to be a bad mother. As part of the nuclear family ideal, the role of the mother and the importance of properly performed maternal duties has been lauded by a whole range of experts, from health visitors, to teachers, child psychologists and a whole sector of the media industry. In sharp contrast a bad mother is one who deviates from full-time motherhood, but the worst sort of bad mother is the single-parent mother (Rose, 1999: 216). This concept of the bad mother was given a significant boost in the 1950s as a result of the work of John Bowlby and the development of the 'maternal deprivation' thesis 'in his book *Child Care and the Growth of Love* (1953)' (Chambers, 2001: 53). As a result of Bowlby's work there became a growing concern about the detrimental impact on a child's emotional development, where they experienced any separation from the mother, including in particular, if children were placed in day nurseries or with persons other than the mother, for example, aunts, grandparents, especially if the mother was leaving her child to be reared by others simply because she wished go out to work.

The notion of maternal deprivation not only became a cultural norm, but also influenced public policy to the point where, in America, day-care provision was refused to women who were supplementing a family income on the grounds that it was wrong for babies to be separated from their mothers at any time (Chambers, 2001: 54), although this disregarded the need of those families where mothers had no choice but to go out to work. Maternal deprivation is also often cited as the cause for juvenile delinquency and a range of other behaviours that can be attributed to the 'demon child' (Muncie, 2004). In this way, we see not only how the idea of bad mothering becomes associated with mothers who go out to work, and because it is the poorest women who need to work and they are often working-class and non-white, the label of bad mother by default translates to women in these sectors in society.

A further example of the bad parent is 'the teenage mother, particularly the single teenage mother' (Wyness, 1999: 11). 'Teenage mothers often have fragile relationships with their partners and 50% of such relationships have ended by the time their baby is one year old' (DfES, 2007c: 3). In 2006 (the most recent data for these statistics) 39,003 young women under 18, in England, became pregnant and approximately 51 per cent went on to have their babies. Approximately one-third (7,296) were women under 16, and 60.3 per cent of these pregnancies ended in a termination of the pregnancy (Every Child Matters, 2008). Most young woman who get pregnant have mothers who also became pregnant at a similar age. For these reasons, it is recognized that where there is support for the whole family this cycle is less likely to be perpetuated. It is also the case that where settings and schools have successfully engaged children, from the very earliest age, in appropriate personal and social education (PSE) education – and engaged children in their learning – young women are more likely to see an alternative to relationships and early pregnancy as a 'way-out'.

Case study

Young and pregnant – YAP

Many Children's Centres run groups to support young women who are pregnant. This case study outlines the help available to young pregnant women through Children's Centres. Claire was 15 when she became pregnant and it was her health visitor who suggested she go to the YAP group at her nearest Children's Centre.

Claire had a good relationship with her baby's father, Tom, and they wanted to be together to bring the baby up. However, initially they lived 50 miles from each other. When Claire was 16 she moved to be with Tom. However, the couple did find being young and pregnant put a huge strain on their relationship and it was under further strain as Tom did not have a job and Claire had moved away from her support network.

Through attending the YAP group Claire was able to make friends with other young mums and to build relationships with the staff at the Centre. As they got to know Claire the staff became more aware of Claire's and Tom's situation and they were able to provide support for Tom through Job Centre Plus to help him get a job. Once the baby was born the Centre continued to provide health-care support for Claire and the baby and, when Claire was ready, they could provide day-care facilities to look after the baby to enable Claire to continue her education.

Families in the wider social context

While we have mainly been focusing on what families might look like. We have also spent considerable effort in exploring the important functions that families perform. However, recent research suggests that not only does the child need to be appropriately cared for and nurtured within a family context, but that a child will flourish better depending on the support the family can also draw on from the wider social context it is in. It is increasingly recognized that many factors impact on the development of a child, the 'child-care center, school, and neighborhood; community resources for child rearing (such as family-friendly workplace policies and high-quality, affordable child care); and cultural values and customs related to child development and education' (Berk, 2004: 22). In particular, the work of Bronfenbrenner stresses the importance of the wider social context and the support it can offer in enabling the well-being of the child, in part through its direct impact on the child, but also through the support it can offer the whole family.

Bronfenbrenner's ecological environment model

1. *'The basic unit is the dyad, the parent–child relationship.'* This is impacted on by the wider social system in which the dyad lives. *'These complex interrelationships form "microsystems".'* Microsystems are patterns of relationships and activities.
2. *'Microsystems rest within "mesosystems". A mesosystem consists of the interrelations among two or more settings in which the developing person participates, such as the home, school and neighbourhood.'*
3. Mesosystems exist within an 'exosystem'. The exosystem is the wider social context that impacts on the mesosystem and microsystem. *'Components of the exosystem include the extended family, parents' workplaces, the mass media, community services and the educational system; the availability and quality of each of these may have implications for how a given family and its microsystems are organised.'*
4. Mesosystems are impacted on by the 'macrosystem', the belief systems and ideologies of the culture, which constitutes a pervasive set of values around which societal life is organized. (Empson, 2004: 30)

The work of Bronfenbrenner is important as it serves to show that while the family is integral to the well-being of the child, the child is part of wider society and that there is a reciprocal relationship between the two. It is the family who in the first instance have primary care for the child, but as the child grows and develops the child naturally wishes to engage more extensively with the wider world, and the society needs children if society is to thrive. Part of achieving well-being is having a fulfilling life in a wider social context; indeed this is recognized in the fourth ECM outcome – making a positive contribution. For children to be able to achieve this relationship with their community they need to be enabled to engage with that community; part of the responsibility for this rests with the family, but Bronfrenbrenner suggests that part of that responsibility rests with the community itself. That the values, attitudes and beliefs a child grows up with are not only as a result of what they have learnt from their family, but from their immediate community too. In this way, as settings and school that form part of the child's mesosystem and, to an extent their macrosystem, we have a very central role to play in the nurturing of children.

Early Years settings and schools

While 'parents and the home environment they create are the single most important factor in shaping their children's well-being, achievements and prospects' (DfES, 2007c: 1) as seen from the Bronnfenbrenner's model above, factors in the wider social context – in this instance the Early Years setting and the school – have huge impact on the child's eventual well-being too, and this is recognized in the ECM agenda, which therefore charges settings and schools to not only ensure children enjoy and achieve in terms of their learning, but are involved in all aspects of enabling them to achieve well-being. And it is also why the ECM agenda recognizes parents do not have to 'bring up' their children alone; raising a child is the work of the whole community.

In its 2007 document, *Every Parent Matters*, the government reiterates and supports the discussion about what constitutes families, which we have explored in this chapter, agreeing that families do not, and do not need to, adhere to the nuclear family model. The document (DfES, 2007c) acknowledges that in most family units all adults need to work to support the family. It recognizes the importance, therefore, of good childcare provision. It also acknowledges the impact of technological, economic, demographic and cultural change that has occurred in Britain over the past 50 years and the challenges that these changes pose to family groups and, particularly, to parents. While changes in the economy, society and technology mean that 'children and young people today have more opportunities than previous generations' (DfES, 2007c: 4) ... Parents can be unsure about how to manage the fine balance between fostering independence and relaxing boundaries while remaining warm and authoritative' (DfES, 2007c: 3). This is an important document since, because it outlines public policy and the models of what constitutes families, family life and parenting it describes and supports, will become the dominant discourse with regard to these concepts.

Every Parent Matters (DfES, 2007c) also outlines what the government regards as good practice in Early Years settings and schools, in terms of settings and schools supporting families and working to develop their home–setting–school links with families. The good practice it cites is drawn from case studies of settings and schools that are working well in this area of their provision.

Case study 📁

As we explored in Chapter 1, society is made up of many groups and cultures, and in some instances, where there is a perceived hierarchy in the grouping, those groups that have more real or perceived power can wittingly or unwittingly dominate and patronize other groups.

At times Early Years settings and schools have been guilty of believing that they know what is best in terms of children's needs and how children should be parented. They have also been seen to belittle some of the challenges parents' are facing and to be dismissive of parents' concerns. Over the past few years much has been done by settings and schools to change this perception of their approach. Below is an example of how a sensitive and thoughtful approach to the challenges one parent was facing have made a significant impact on the lives of one family.

John was very eager to be involved in all aspects of his young children's lives, and was keen to become involved in all the activities offered by the local Children's Centre. After one of his visits with his children a support worker suggested he came to the fathers' group. John was pleased to be asked and duly came along to the next meeting.

At the meeting, without giving it much thought, as the dads arrived the support worker gave out registration forms and asked the dads to provide contact details and other helpful information. When John was given his form he seemed to become quite distressed. Since the support worker knew John and had already built up a relationship with him she felt able to take him to one side and ask him what was wrong. John could not read or write and was upset that, once again, in a place where he felt welcomed and was with people he trusted, he had been humiliated. Upset by her own lack of thought, but thinking on her feet, the support worker took the form from John and said that since he was a regular at the centre, she needed his help to sort out the refreshments and welcome the dads who had not been to the centre before.

John was very pleased to take up this role, he felt valued and needed, and from this episode and disclosure the centre was able to encourage John to join a family learning support programme.

Examples of Early Years settings' and schools' good practice in supporting families

Government research (DfES, 2007c: 9) has shown

> that what parents do is more important than who parents are. Parents engaging in a range of activities with their child has been shown to have an impact on children gaining higher intellectual and social/behavioural scores. These activities included:
>
> - reading with their child;
> - teaching songs and nursery rhymes;
> - painting and drawing;
> - playing with letters and numbers;

continued

continued

- visiting the library, museums and other places; as well as
- creating regular opportunities to play with friends. (DfES, 2007c: 9)

Settings and schools that have appreciated that some parents have issues with numeracy and literacy have been very successful in engaging parents in their children's learning and development where they have worked with parents to provide family learning programmes. 'They also boost parents' involvement in their children's learning, encourage parents to go on to further training and can re-connect them with schools they might previously have been wary of' (DfES, 2007c: 11).

Many settings and schools have adopted successful practice from Children's Centres, particularly in developing the role of an outreach worker, or community liaison worker. Where schools have developed this role, it is often an experienced teaching assistant that has taken on the responsibility. The advantage of having someone whose sole role is to go out into the community helps to build relationships in the local area and – 'while at all times respecting parents' wishes – focus on ensuring that those families not taking up the offer are doing so out of choice' (DfES, 2007c: 11). Outreach work is particularly successful as:

> outreach services and home visiting – giving special attention to those families that need extra help with their children. The blend of services delivered in each centre is informed by consultation with parents, children and the community, as well as demographic data on likely local needs. Ongoing responsiveness to parents' and children's needs. (DfES, 2007c: 14)

Further reading

Department for Education and Skills (DfES) (2003) *Materials for Schools: Involving parents, raising achievement*. London: DfES.

Department for Education and Skills (DfES) (2007c) *Every Parent Matters*. London: DfES.

Peters, M., Seeds, K., Goldstein, A. and Coleman, N. (2008) *Parental Involvement in Children's Education 2007*. BMRB International Ltd/DCSF.

Useful websites

www.fatherhoodinstitute.org/

www.everychildmatters.gov.uk

Being Healthy

> This chapter explores:
>
> - what it means for children to be physically, mentally and emotionally healthy;
> - that the concept of health includes physical, mental and emotional health;
> - the notion of resilience and understanding how resilience can help children and families better achieve the five outcomes for well-being; and
> - how the issues of sexual health and choosing not to take illegal drugs can be introduced in Early Years settings and primary schools.

The *Every Child Matters Outcomes Framework* (DCSF, 2008b) for enabling children and families to be healthy requires that Early Years settings and primary schools must demonstrate that they are enabling children to be in an environment that allows them to enjoy physical, mental and emotional health. Settings and schools also have a duty to ensure children learn how to achieve these things for themselves and live healthy lifestyles, and that they understand what it is to be sexually healthy and choose not to take illegal drugs.

Physical health

Over the past few years there has been increasing concern about the health of children, and the government feels there is evidence to suggest too few children enjoy the right diet and levels of physical activity needed to keep them healthy (DfES, 2004c). For these reasons the government is looking to settings and schools to take the lead in helping children and their families enjoy a healthy lifestyle and adopt practices that will ensure they continue to do this in the long term. Through setting good examples and teaching children through the curriculum and through its polices and practices, settings and schools can engage children in physical activity and make informed choices about what to eat and drink. Settings and schools are also well placed to provide children and families with other health-care support as needed, modelling the good multi-agency practice already being used in Children Centres (DfES, 2004c). In its document *Healthy Living Blueprint for Schools* (DfES, 2004c) the government charges settings and schools to:

1. develop an ethos and culture within the setting or school that promotes and encourages a healthy lifestyle;
2. use the learning opportunities already part of the curriculum documentation to teach children about healthy lifestyles;
3. ensure that any food or drink available to children across the setting or school day is healthy;
4. ensure children have the opportunity to engage in physical activity; and
5. 'promote an understanding of the full range of issues and behaviours which impact upon lifelong health' (DfES, 2004c).

In terms of specific guidance to Early Years settings, the government states that

- fresh drinking water should be available to children at all times
- children who stay in day care for the whole day are offered a midday meal and other healthy snacks and drinks routinely
- the provider requests information from parents about any special dietary requirements, preferences or food allergies the child may have and
- if parents provide packed lunches, they are informed of what can be stored away safely. (DfES, 2004c)

It is no accident that the first of the five ECM outcomes for well-being is that of 'being healthy'. It has long been recognized that children's physical, mental and emotional health will have a huge impact on how children and families can access the other opportunities that the ECM agenda makes available to them (NHSP, 2008: 1) and, in this instance, the proven link between a child's good health, behaviour and their educational achievement.

There is considerable guidance available to practitioners, teachers and others about what constitutes healthy eating and appropriate physical activity. Much of this information can be found at www.healthyschools.gov.uk. Where settings and schools can feel more vulnerable, in terms of helping children and families to meet the 'be healthy' outcome, is in supporting and promoting mental and emotional health, and this, therefore, is the focus of this chapter.

Emotional health and well-being

The Healthy Schools website that discusses the importance of mental and emotional health, states that: 'the promotion of positive emotional health and well-being helps children and young people to understand and express their feelings, build their confidence and emotional resilience, and therefore their capacity to learn' (Emotional Health and Well-being, 2008). It is becoming increasingly widely recognized that children whose emotional health issues go undetected – or children who are not enabled to be resilient in dealing with mental and emotional stressors – may later develop ongoing mental health problems as adults (Dwivedi, 2004: 15). Below are a number of mental health problems which children can suffer. However, the information given here is to alert practitioners, teacher and other to the fact that even very young children can suffer mental health problems. In no way is the information to be read as a diagnosis of a child's health issue. Where you are concerned about a child you must seek expert help and guidance.

Depression and anxiety disorders

There are concerns that the numbers of children and young people diagnosed with depression and anxiety disorders is increasing, and the number of children who are experiencing problems that are going undiagnosed or not treated effectively is of particular worry since there is a correlation between the length of time a child takes to recover from a condition and the likelihood of the condition recurring – the longer the recovery period, the more likely a repeat episode. More concerning still, is the correlation between adolescent depression, anxiety disorders and suicide rates. Research shows that up to 20 per cent of all children will suffer with some form of anxiety disorder, although for many children these may be of short duration and occasioned by particular, easily identifiable events such as a problem at home, worries about school and friends or being overly concerned about forthcoming tests and examinations (CAMHS, 2008: 7; March, 2004). In some children the anxiety persists and can develop into a debilitating disorder or depression. In these instances there is often a more persistent underlying factor that is the cause of the anxiety. For those children, some of the main factors contributing to the likelihood of depression and anxiety are:

- perceived pressures to achieve/conform/behave in certain ways and meet particular expectations, either from external sources of from the child themselves;
- experiences of loneliness and isolation;
- physical, sexual and emotional abuse;
- feelings of insecurity relating to issues of attachment, from an early age;
- parents who suffer from depression, anxiety disorders, or have drug and alcohol problems;
- experiences of loss and unsupported bereavement at an early age;
- tensions arising from issues related to the child's ethnicity; and
- issues associated with poverty and deprivation (Dwivedi, 2004; March, 2004).

Perhaps not surprisingly, children who experience depression and anxiety disorders will often have – or will develop – self-esteem issues and generally have a more hopeless attitude towards life and future possibilities.

However, the problem mostly 'untrained' practitioners and teachers have is knowing how to determine between normal anxiety responses to a stressful situation and when the child's response becomes a cause for concern. Dwivedi (2004) suggests a possible warning signal might be that the child's response to a situation seems out of proportion to what might be a more expected response, that the child's response begins to interfere with other day-to-day pursuits and that the anxiety persists over a significant period of time, for example, beyond when the anxiety-inducing event has happened. A further way of determining the scale of the child's condition is where the child is particularly shy or withdrawn and focuses on particular repetitive thoughts or exhibits repetitive behaviours. A child who has depression or anxiety may also be unable to sleep, lose interest in food does not seem motivated to concentrate on any activities, may stop talking or lose interest in their friends and playing (March, 2004).

Eating disorders

Eating disorders occur for very complex reasons and again, there may be no single cause. Generally it is thought those suffering with eating disorders are using food as a way of coping with other emotions that are too challenging to confront directly, or for other reasons have to be hidden or suppressed (Michel, 2003: 2). It is still unclear what causes young people to develop eating disorders but research has shown that risk factors can develop in childhood and include a poor body/self-image, a tendency to want everything to be perfect or, again, low self-esteem. There is also evidence that eating disorders can go hand-in-hand with anxiety disorders and depression. It is also possible to cite research that claims the media's portrayal of particularly thin body shapes as being desirable in women; the perceived breakdown of the traditional family, resulting in lack of formally available support systems for children and young people; and the notion of rapid cultural and moral change that leaves children and young people adrift in terms of having a system of beliefs and attitudes to support them and to fall back on, are also contributing factors. Research also finds a correlation between mothers who are concerned with their weight and dieting and the increased risk of daughters developing eating disorders; peer pressure and peer relationships and the pursuit of activities such as athletics and gymnastics can be a high-risk factor in terms of who might develop eating disorders (Dwivedi, 2004; Michel, 2003).

Prevention

While the research differs on stating what might be the most high-risk single cause of eating disorders, the link that does bind them all is that of low self-esteem. Children who have high self-esteem are less likely to develop eating disorders. Other factors that have been found as key to prevention of eating disorders are: positive family relationships; high levels of support from fathers; a more accepting peer group, particularly with regard to tolerance of difference and being involved in an interest which the child or young person finds absorbing and fulfilling (Dwivedi, 2004: 178). Michel (2004) suggests that some young people develop eating disorders because the disorder actually acts to boost the lacking self-esteem. Being able to control food intake, either by restricting the amount of food eaten or through inducing vomiting to get rid of food already consumed, can induce the feeling of being in control and therefore boost confidence. It may also be the case that the sufferer gains more attention through having a disorder and this can make the young person feel less lonely and marginalized.

Activity

Below are a number of activities to try with children to raise self-esteem.

What makes me feel good/feel bad
Sometimes children need help to separate out what it is that makes them feel good – or bad. If they can learn to predict what their reaction is likely to be to something you are going to expect them to do, they will be better placed to know when to ask for help – and you will know when they are likely to need support.

They will also know what it is that makes them feel good and this can be used as a strategy by you and the child to build on developing positive self-esteem and help the child understand that they do have some control over their feelings and managing tasks they are being asked to complete.

Depending on the age of the children you are working with and how many children you are working with, the activity outlined below can be adapted to suit your situation.

The activity is based around gaining the child or children's response to the following sorts of statements:

- I felt bad when I wanted to tell my key worker/teacher what I got for my birthday/my auntie was coming/I got a new pair of trainers, but they were too busy to listen.
- I felt really good when I got a sticker for my ... work.
- I felt bad when I fell out with ... at playtime.
- I felt good when I built a really big ... with the ... .
- I felt bad when my mum cried last night.
- I felt good when my sister got a good report from school.

You can make up your own statements to suit the context you are in. Start the session by talking about yourself – when you felt good/bad.

Where possible, encourage the children to talk about how they can protect themselves from feeling bad, or recover the situation. Simply having the space to talk about what makes them feel bad will help, and if you can encourage them to come up with their own strategies for feeling good, they will feel more empowered and in control of the situation.

Case study

Often where there seems to be ill feeling or conflict between children it is because the children have not, for whatever reason, developed strategies for being in large groups alongside others, or they are not able to read another's body language, or the strategies that they have learnt are not appropriate for the setting or school situation.

Sometimes children need to be taught how to behave in groups – turn-taking, listening to what others have to say and responding appropriately. Sometimes children will take an 'instant' dislike to another child, for no apparent reason and this will lead to ongoing conflict.

In many cases these types of issues can be addressed by providing the children with the time and space, and sometimes a directed activity, to talk things over.

For example, Craig an 11-year-old boy in a Midlands primary school had difficulty in playing with the other children. He would get angry if things did not go the way he wanted and the other children would refuse to play with him. Craig's parents had split up and he was living with his little sister and his mum at his mum's new boyfriend's house. The class had a regular circle time session and in one session where they were asked to name one thing that went well this week – then one thing that did not. In this session Craig told the class that he had been in town at the weekend with his mum, her boyfriend and his sister and that they had bumped into his dad. Craig wanted desperately to go to his dad and talk to him, but his mum forbade him to do so.

As Craig reported this episode, which he did in a fairly matter-of-fact way, the reaction on the faces of many of the other children was very noticeable. They wanted to ask Craig more questions about the incident, which he was happy to answer. The change in the other children's acceptance of Craig after this event was also very marked and this, in turn, made Craig less aggressive towards them.

'Breakthroughs' like this will happen in circle time sessions and can be very powerful, but they only occur after a group has been working together for a while and a level of trust has built up – including trust in you as the adult managing these sessions.

Children and Adolescent Mental Health Service (CAMHS)

Where there are concerns about a child's mental or emotional health and whether or not these are referred through a health worker or General Practitioner, it is likely that the child and family will be put in touch with the nearest branch of the Children and Adolescent Mental Health Service.

The Children and Adolescent Mental Health Service is a specialist service for children and young people who have mental health problems. It is recognized that up to one in ten children or young people may sufferer with mental health problems and, being so young benefit greatly from working with staff specially trained to help children, and they work with children and young people up to the age of 16. When a child is referred to them they will contact the child's parents, by letter, to offer an initial appointment. The letter may request that the appointment is just for the child or it might request that the parent/carer attend – or the whole family. Children and Adolescent Mental Health Service teams may work from their own clinics, or they may make home visits, or come to the setting or school, or be available at the local doctors' surgery. 'People working in CAMHS are all trained in mental health and include: psychiatrists, nurses, social workers, psychologists, psychotherapists, family therapists, teachers, primary mental health workers and community outreach workers.' When they have made their initial assessment they may recommend: 'different forms of therapy, medication (though this is not common)' and how many appointments they think the child needs, perhaps one or two or weekly appointments for a few weeks. In very rare cases it may be recommended that hospital is the best place for the child. (Care Services and Improvement Partnership, 2008).

Resilience

The notion of resilience is increasingly being recognized as important to child and family emotional and mental health. The understanding of what resilience is has come from research that tracked the long-term well-being of children who might, from the circumstances of their childhoods, be expected – given dominant discourses – to lead dysfunctional lives as adults. What has been found is that many children 'who suffered childhood adversity defied dire expectations of serious and long-lasting damage, instead growing up to lead full, loving, and productive lives' (Walsh, 2006: 4). Traditionally the notion of resilience has been of an almost fool-hardiness in carrying on in the face of adversity and was seen as something that was an innate personality trait, found in only some people. However, it is now seen as something which, with the right support, most individuals and families have and can utilize to see them through difficult and challenging stressors. It is about building on the positive factors that are present in any situation and using these to strengthen the individual or family overall (Glantz, 1999).

When a family is facing a challenge, a divorce for example, whereas before this has been seen as an event that might cause the family to 'break down' and may lead to other forms of dysfunctional family behaviour, support is directed to target what are the key problems resulting from the breakup and what resources the family themselves have that can be utilized to cope with the situation. For some children and families the challenges are of a long-term nature, for others many challenges that stress individuals and families do so because they involve some form of change. Change can be adapted to, and indeed is sometimes wanted and eagerly anticipated, but it is more challenging to deal with if it is unwanted or unexpected. Sudden and unexpected change can be difficult for children to deal with as they have a more limited range of contexts and experiences to draw on to help them deal with the situation. As we get older we have more experience and tried and tested coping strategies to draw on.

One of the greatest stressors a child may face is the death of a parent. Helping a child deal with this situation is, in part, about helping the child adapt to the changes that will now happen in their lives. While the child will be experiencing considerable grief at losing their parent, the way they are feeling may also be exacerbated by other concerns, some which they might not be able to name or articulate. In situations like this children also worry about things like, who will make the tea? Where will I live? How will I get to school? How do I help other people in my family be happy again? Even worries such as, will I still have birthday presents? Who will make sure there is cat food to feed the cat? Adults wishing to comfort children in such circumstances can be very good at being affectionate and loving towards them, but very often children want very practical help too.

If a child can be given the opportunity to talk through and 'sort out' the different issues they feel faced with in the situation, it is sometimes possible to solve, very simply, some of the worries a child has. Most often the worries will be about what is going to happen next, how things are going to change and what is going to happen in the future. Helping children articulate these concerns can make the child feel empowered and give them back some control over what may be a very confusing and overwhelming situation; it gives the child permission to still worry about having birthday presents, and the understanding that worrying about these things does not mean that they miss the lost parent any the less. If the child can be given strategies to cope with some of the more pragmatic aspects of the situation, they will be more able to deal with the more challenging aspects – like the grief they feel. In these ways children can be taught to be resilient, to learn that while some situations seem overwhelming, with support they can be dealt with. In the same way, it is possible to work with families in challenging situations to help them use the resilience they have or to help them develop resilience (Daniel and Wassell, 2002a).

Resilience is a very helpful notion for both the children and families that are facing challenges, and for those working with them to overcome the challenges, since research in this area acknowledges that while the immediate issues thrown up by any challenging situation will have an impact on the child and family, with support both can recover and that 'the events that go wrong in our lives do not forever damn us' (Glantz, 1999; Walsh, 2006: 9).

Individuals have been shown to be particularly resilient when:

- that individual believes they have some influence and control over the events in their lives;
- they feel committed to some form of activity in their lives;
- they can see change as being an exciting possibility;
- moral and spiritual convictions can be sources of support; and
- they have the self-confidence to know that things can get better and problems can be overcome, even if some aspects of them will not go away (Glantz, 1999; Walsh, 2006).

Much of the research into resilience comes from work with children who have 'survived' seemingly 'chaotic' childhoods (Glanzt, 1999; Walsh, 2006). The research shows that these children were resilient to the possible stressors in their lives because they had an innate sense of their own worth, or because others had worked with them to help them gain this selfworth – this and a sense of control in shaping their futures helped them overcome these early obstacles. Importantly for those working with children and families and seeking to support them through difficult life events, Walsh (2006) believes it is possible for optimism to be learnt, just as helplessness can be a learnt response. Just as people can learn to be passive and give up, particularly if they see any efforts they believe they have made failing to result in a wanted outcome, so too by working with children and families to set manageable targets and help them realize goals they can begin to develop the skills, knowledge, understanding and belief that they do have control over shaping events in their lives.

One of the single most important features in helping a child be resilient, or develop resilience, is the presence of at least one supportive significant adult in their lives (Daniel and Wassell, 2002a; Hoffman, 2004; Walsh, 2006). In part this is because such a relationship provides the experience of being accepted and loved unconditionally, which is invaluable in helping a child develop self-esteem and a sense of worth. This is also why peer-mentoring and 'buddying' systems can work so well with children experiencing difficulties at school. Other providers of strong relationships that foster resilience are:

• family members from the extended family, including older siblings, grand-parents; and
• friends, neighbours, teachers, coaches, clergy and other mentors, who can have a positive impact in enabling a child to develop resilience (Berk, 2004).

When a child is very young, it may be difficult for those who wish to support the child to be able to fully interpret what the child's needs or concerns are. In such instances research shows that what seems to help the child is ensuring systematic, routine care strategies are in place, as 'often simple strategies, applied with persistence and consistency, can strengthen the child's feeling of basic security and belonging' (Daniel and Wassell, 2002: 87). Indeed, one of the greatest benefits settings and schools provide in generally supporting and helping all children's and families' resilience is that they are always there, they have a routine and they are consistent. A child or family coming to a setting or school knows what to expect, there are rarely any really negative surprises and usually they are caring welcoming places. Settings and schools should not be cavalier in dismissing this vital element of support they provide.

Families at particular risk of being overlooked and not supported

In all the work that has been done in developing support for vulnerable children and families there are still particular groups that tend to be overlooked. In 2007 the DfES highlighted particular concern for children who are carers of parents, possibly because their parents may be disabled, have other physical and mental health issues or have drug/alcohol abuse problems. The DfES states: 'disabled children are often in the poorest families and face real barriers to full participation and attainment' (DfES, 2007c: 14). Settings and schools need to be particularly alert to the needs of children in these situations.

Activity

One of the recurring themes of this chapter is how important self-esteem is to children's mental health.

Below are some further activities to try with children to help promote self-esteem.

How important am I?

Sometimes children feel marginalized and overlooked. This can exacerbate any feelings of isolation or of being marginalized that they may already be experiencing. Sometimes these feelings are engendered by things happening at home, which you will not necessarily be able to influence.

However, sometimes, in the setting or school, we can be guilty of overlooking certain children, or always asking the seemingly competent and reliable ones to do things for us.

There are many ways to help children feel important – often just having time to reflect on how we work with children will immediately make us think 'tomorrow I must ask Charlie to … and not always rely on Saelisha to …', or 'if I ask Kirsten and Somy to … together, Somy can show Kirsten how to do it for next time'.

You may want to undertake an activity that provides the opportunity for children to articulate when they feel important, or unimportant. When you do these activities it is always a good idea to have some statements prepared to get you started and for you to model what you are after.

Starting statements:

- I felt important when I was asked to take a message to the school office.
- I do not feel important because I am always being told off for being slow getting changed after PE.
- I felt important when Mrs Barnard said my painting was very good.
- I do not feel important because I am never allowed to hand the fruit around.

It is always very powerful in these activities if you can model the activity by saying something that made you feel important, or unimportant; for example:

- I felt important when Mr King said my children were working hard.
- I did not feel important when Mrs Barnard said I was late back from playtime.

Again, where you can help children develop strategies for dealing with these situations you can increase their sense of worth and control over situations.

Too often in working with families we have been guilty of using a deficit model, that is, we know when something is 'wrong', but not when something is going alright. It also means we tend only to focus on those families who are experiencing problems and look for trends of similarity. One of those trends may be that the families experiencing problems are single-parent families, but that may be a symptom of problems – not the cause. It also means we do not know how many single-parent families are doing well and, indeed, what problems they have already successfully overcome to reach where they are now.

It is what enables families to cope, that makes them resilient. Focusing on 'problems' reinforces the notion of the ideal healthy family, since no research, until recently, has been done on those families that are resilient the myth that only the idealized 'nuclear' family is successful, has been allowed to be perpetuated. As Walsh (2006) states, because those families who have problems become the ones who are noticed, set against the myth of the problem-free nuclear family, we know that all sorts of family groups can be successful. It is not having the ideal family unit of the nuclear family that, of itself makes families successful, it is the effectiveness of their strategies for dealing with challenges and solving problems that life throws up for them. Therefore, we must look at the factors in a range of healthy – or resilient – well-functioning families that provide us with the trends to support how families thrive, that is, a 'strength-orientated' model not a 'deficit-based' model (Daniel and Wassell, 2002a; Walsh, 2006).

In a stressful situation, those families that are resilient, or develop their resilience as part of dealing with and surviving that stress, are those who are supported through the difficulties by being provided with strategies to mitigate or deal with the stressor. That is, the families are taught how to deal with the situation, they learn that things can be dealt with and overcome, that they do not have to be at the mercy of the stressor. This will serve to strengthen them for the next stressor, realizing that situations change and some eventually end and some can be mitigated and controlled. Resilience is not something static; it is responsive to situations and can be developed.

Personal, social and health education

The final objective of this chapter is to explore how settings and schools can ensure that they meet the aspect of the *be healthy* ECM aim that deals with issues of sexual health and choosing not to take illegal drugs. For some settings and schools this can seem a requirement too far. However, both the Early Years Foundation Stage framework and the National Curriculum for primary school children contains personal, social and health education in one form or another, and it is mainly in these areas of the curriculum that the subjects of sex and substance abuse are dealt with. The strength of having these issues in the curriculum documentation means that they can be approached in ways appropriate to the age of the children, and that help and guidance is available to help settings and schools in dealing with, what can be, challenging subjects. It is also important to consider that where children have appropriate knowledge and understanding about sex and the problems that can be caused by drugs and alcohol, they are more likely to be kept safe from harm associated with sexual activity or drug and alcohol use. This is something that is dealt with at more length in the following chapter.

Sex education in the Early Years and in the primary school

In Britain and America, particularly, we give children very mixed messages about sex. For example, in writing in this area, Levine (2004) talks of the 'clean-up' of Times Square in New York, she writes about the removing of the neon signs advertising 'peep-shows' only to have them replaced by 'half-block-long billboards [that] advertised Calvin Klein underwear, inside of whose painted shadows lurked penises as large as redwood logs' (Levine, 2002: 4). As a society we have a dominant discourse about what might be termed sexuality, rather than sex. There is a strong drive, fuelled by the media and the fashion industry, that stresses the importance of being a sexually attractive and sexually active adult. The 'leakage' from this adult arena seeps out into the domain of children. They too know that sex is out there and it is something that adults find very compelling; however, we have yet to learn how to induct children into this area of adult life in a way that protects them from its more harmful side, and enables them to take on its complexity in a measured way.

In almost all other areas of children's growth, development and learning we celebrate curiosity and encourage children to ask questions and experiment with ideas and applaud them for taking risks – except when it comes to sex. In part this is because when the word 'sex' is mentioned, in our thinking we skip any other aspects associated with the term and move immediately to the act of 'having sex' itself. In discussing what sex might be, and particularly when we are talking about sex education, we seem to assume that it is only the act of having sex that we are considering and only this which will be discussed with children, and that they will either be distressed by the revelations of what the act of having sex entails, or they will promptly – at whatever age – go out and 'try it themselves'. While there is no doubt that 'learning about sex affects what a person does and feels about it' (Levine, 2002: 8), it also follows that how a child learns about it and what they learn will influence how they then choose to deal with this knowledge and understanding.

For many there is a concern that the dominant discourses surrounding sex seems to separate out the act of having sex from the notion of a trusting relationship within which the act is an act of love and trust, not something of itself. Let us briefly explore the notion of relationship. The very idea of a relationship is that it is something that builds up over time, and it is part of the development of a mutually fulfilling and successful relationship that, as part of the relationship, trust between the people in the relationship develops. In certain circumstances, which also require a level of emotional and physical maturity, the relationship may become a sexual one. This does not ignore the very serious issue of child sexual abuse, that is, those who will deliberately court a seemingly trusting relationship and subsequently abuse their position in the relationship; or those that will coerce a child who is not emotionally, physically or legally mature enough to engage in a sexual act. This is dealt with in Chapter 5, in terms of children being safe. What we are concerned with here is how, in the best course of events, children learn about sex and sexual relationships in a way that is fulfilling for them – as is age appropriate.

If we return to the notion of relationships and what constitutes a healthy relationship, we can then move on to taking these concepts as being the starting point for the act of having sex, as part of particular kinds of relationships. The Personal, Social and Emotional Development early learning goals of the Early Years Foundation Stage framework (EYFS) provide for exactly this to happen. In working with children in this area of their development practitioners need to help children:

- develop a positive sense of themselves and of others;
- develop respect for others;
- show a range of feelings when appropriate;
- develop an awareness of their own needs, views and feelings, and be sensitive to the needs, views and feelings of others;
- form good relationships with adults and peers; and
- understand what is right and wrong, and consider consequences of their words and actions for themselves and others (DfES, 2007a: 12).

The early learning goal Knowledge and Understanding of the World states that children should have the opportunity to:

- find out about past and present events in their own lives, and those of their families and other people they know; and
- begin to know about their own cultures and beliefs and those of other people (DfES, 2007a: 15).

All these learning experiences are to enable children to develop a sense of themselves and themselves in relation to others. Part of the knowledge and understanding children are acquiring through the early learning goals is the foundations of the necessary knowledge and understanding needed to eventually build those relationships within which sex will occur.

The themes outlined above from the EYFS are further developed through the primary phase of the National Curriculum. The NC non-statutory guidance for personal, social and health education and citizenship (PSHE and citizenship), states that children between the ages of 5 and 7 should have the opportunity to:

- recognize what they like and dislike, what is fair and unfair, and what is right and wrong;
- to recognize, name and deal with feelings in a positive way;
- to make simple choices that improve their health and well-being;
- learn about the process of growing from young to old and how people's needs change;
- learn the names of the main parts of the body;

- to recognize how their behaviour affects other people; and
- recognize that family and friends should care for each other.

While between the ages of 8 to 11, children should have the opportunity to further build on this knowledge and understanding, deepening this by learning:

- to recognize their worth as individuals;
- to recognize, as they approach puberty, how people's emotions change;
- to explore how the media present information;
- what makes a healthy lifestyle and how to make informed choices;
- that pressure to behave in an unacceptable or risky way can come from a variety of sources, including people they know and where to go to ask for help;
- judging what kind of physical contact is acceptable or unacceptable; and
- to be aware of different types of relationship (DfES/QCA, 1999: 137–40).

Through these aspects of required learning activities we can see how there is considerable scope for much work to be done with children about helping them develop a sense of self and what relationships are about. Alongside this aspect of the curriculum, what is traditionally seen as 'sex education', that is, what is usually seen as explaining to children the act of human reproduction, forms part of the science programme of study in the National Curriculum. In science, between the ages of 5 and 7 children learn:

- to recognize and compare the main external parts of the bodies of human and other animals; and
- that humans and other animals can produce offspring and that these offspring grow into adults.

For children between the ages of 8 and 11, this aspect of knowledge and understanding develops into:

- life processes common to humans include growth and reproduction;
- about the main stages of the human lifecycle (DfES/QCA, 1999: 79 and 85).

In exploring these issues, Levine (2002) highlights the challenges and dilemmas faced by adults working with children and trying to negotiate what can seem like the minefield of relationship and sex education. She states: 'How can we be both realistic and idealistic about sex? With toddlers, children, or adolescents, how can we be protective but not intrusive, instructive but not preachy, serious but not grim, playful but not frivolous?' (Levine, 2002: 138).

Drugs and alcohol education in the Early Years and in the primary school

While it is less common for children in Early Years settings and primary schools to actively seek to consume illegal drugs and alcohol, it is not unheard of.

Neither is it uncommon for children to be subjected to drug and alcohol use or abuse, that is, forced or coerced into taking drugs and alcohol by others, for whatever reasons. This is a recognized form of child abuse and is covered in the following chapter. While, except in the circumstances just outlined, it is unlikely that young children will take drugs or alcohol, they can be at risk because of use or misuse of these substances by parents and older siblings. Research also shows that, where children grow up in a family where drugs and alcohol are misused or there are drug or alcohol addicts in the household, at adolescence the children are more likely to misuse these substances too, since misuse of alcohol and drugs is usually learnt behaviour (Fitzgerald, 2000: 193). 'In terms of substance use and abuse, these are developmental periods of great importance because they represent periods of substance use initiation and escalation. Developmentally, most substance use begins in adolescence, reaches a peak in the mid-20s, and then declines' (Fitzgerald, 2000: 193).

The other risk factors associated with drug and alcohol misuse, especially in young people, are that they escalate the incidents of tragic accidents, criminal behaviour and dangerous sexual practices in the adolescent age group. In the same way as we have seen how the EYFS framework for the early learning goals and the National Curriculum require children to be presented with the opportunity to develop knowledge and understanding about sexual practices, there is the similar provision for children to learn about drugs and alcohol use.

Further reading

Daniel, B. and Wassell, S. (2002a) *Early Years: Assessing and Promoting Resilience in Vulnerable Children*. London: Jessica Kingsley.

Daniel, B. and Wassell, S. (2002b) *Adolescence: Assessing and Promoting Resilience in Vulnerable Children*. London: Jessica Kingsley.

Daniel, B. and Wassell, S. (2002c) *School Years: Assessing and Promoting Resilience in Vulnerable Children*. London: Jessica Kingsley.

Department for Education and Employment (DfEE) (2000) *Sex and Relationship Education Guidance*. London: DfEE.

Office for Standards in Education (OfSTED) (2005a) *Drug Education in Schools*. London: HMI.

Useful websites

www.healthyschools.gov.uk/

Child and Adolescent Mental Health Service: www.camhs.org.uk/

www.teachers.TV – this has some helpful videos about issues raised in this chapter, particularly in relation to teaching about sex and substance abuse.

For information about how to approach substance abuse childline has some useful information on its website: www.childline.org.uk/Info/DamagingYourself/Pages/Drugs

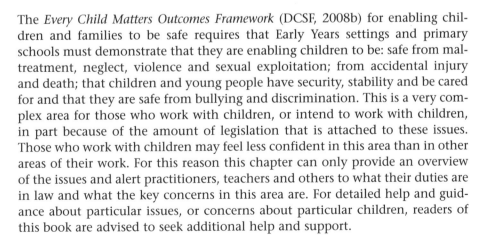

Staying safe

This chapter explores:

- the duty that all who come into contact with children have, in law, to ensure that children are safeguarded from maltreatment;
- what constitutes maltreatment and abuse of children;
- how children can be vulnerable to abuse, particularly sexual abuse and how children can be safeguarded against such abuse;
- the process for reporting suspected abuse and what the outcomes of such reporting might be; and
- ways in which the Early Years Foundation Stage Framework and the National Curriculum provide for children to be taught to be safe.

The *Every Child Matters Outcomes Framework* (DCSF, 2008b) for enabling children and families to be safe requires that Early Years settings and primary schools must demonstrate that they are enabling children to be: safe from maltreatment, neglect, violence and sexual exploitation; from accidental injury and death; that children and young people have security, stability and be cared for and that they are safe from bullying and discrimination. This is a very complex area for those who work with children, or intend to work with children, in part because of the amount of legislation that is attached to these issues. Those who work with children may feel less confident in this area than in other areas of their work. For this reason this chapter can only provide an overview of the issues and alert practitioners, teachers and others to what their duties are in law and what the key concerns in this area are. For detailed help and guidance about particular issues, or concerns about particular children, readers of this book are advised to seek additional help and support.

As with all five aspects of the Every Child Matters (ECM) agenda, settings and schools have a duty, on the one hand, to ensure that, in this instance, they are keeping children safe and, on the other, they are enabling children to develop the skills, knowledge and understanding to keep themselves safe. This chapter explores what constitutes maltreatment, neglect, violence and sexual exploitation, lack of security and stability, bullying and discrimination, and what settings and schools need to do if they suspect any of the above is happening to a child. The chapter also makes some suggestions as to how children can be helped to develop the necessary skills, knowledge and understanding to keep themselves safe.

The Education Act 2002 places a duty on settings and schools to safeguard and promote the welfare of all children, including ensuring they provide a safe environment themselves and take steps, through their policies, practice and training, to identify 'child welfare concerns and take action to address them, in partnership with other organisations where appropriate' (HM Government, 2006: 13). The Education Act 2002 also places this duty on childminders and any organization that provides day care for children – of whatever age.

For the most current guidance on the concerns and issues raised in this chapter, including what your role in safeguarding children is, and where you can go for help, it is strongly recommended that you obtain (free) and read a copy of the Department for Education and Skills document: *What to Do if You Are Worried a Child Is Being Abused* (2006). In this document it states that safeguarding and promoting the welfare of children, as outlined in the statutory guidance under the Children Acts 1989 and 2004, means:

- protecting children from maltreatment;
- preventing impairment of children's health or development;
- ensuring that children are growing up in circumstances consistent with the provision of safe and effective care; and
- undertaking that role so as to enable children to have optimum life chances and to enter adulthood successfully (DfES, 2006: 7).

It is essential that children are safeguarded from maltreatment and impairment of their health and development not only to prevent the terrible day-to-day suffering some children are subjected to, but also to ensure that children are safe from these abuses to protect their long-term well-being (Combrinck-Graham, 2006: 480). Deliberate and sustained maltreatment, which includes physical, emotional and sexual abuse of children is not confined to any particular group or culture; it pervades all groups, classes and cultures. Alongside deliberate or intentional abuse, some children can be recognized as being at risk from unintended harm. Children who also need to be safeguarded from the short-term and the longer-term effects of damaging environments are those children who live in families:

- that are living in poverty
- where there is domestic violence
- where a parent has a mental illness
- where a parent is misusing drugs or alcohol

- where a parent has a learning disability
- that face racism and other forms of social isolation
- living in areas with a lot of crime, poor housing and high unemployment.
(HM Government, 2006: 18)

Children who may be vulnerable and are also classed as suffering abuse include: children living away from home, disabled children, those being abused by other children and young people, those being bullied, children whose behaviour indicates a lack of parental control, those subjected to racism, children accused of 'possession' or 'witchcraft' or in other practices related to spiritual or religious beliefs, abuse through information and communication technology (ICT), children and families who go missing, children of families living in temporary accommodation, migrant children, child victims of trafficking and unaccompanied asylum-seeking children (UASC) (HM Government, 2006: 19).

We cannot also ignore the fact that some children come to this country as refugee and asylum seekers from countries affected by war, where they may be deeply affected by death of close family members and personal injury, and it is also estimated that there are 300,000 children being deployed as soldiers. Children may also arrive from countries where they may have worked as child labourers, have been born with AIDs, have family members who are suffering with the disease, or be here as a result of being trafficked (Corby, 2005: 81).

> Some children are in need because they are suffering or likely to suffer significant harm. The Children Act 1989 introduced the concept of significant harm as the threshold that justifies compulsory intervention in family life in the best interests of children. The local authority is under a duty to make enquiries, or cause enquiries to be made, where it has reasonable cause to suspect that a child is suffering, or likely to suffer, significant harm. (DfES, 2006: 8)

The range of harms that children need to be safeguarded against can seem overwhelming. However, current practice recognizes that while there are children who need immediate and direct intervention to protect them from abuse, others will move in and out of some of the categories listed above as family circumstances change. In reality many children will fall into one of the categories listed above at some point in their childhoods. As we have seen in Chapter 4, where a family's circumstances are under a particular stress or set of stressors at any one time, what our role might be is to help to support to reduce the stressor and offer strategies to build resilience to withstand and move on from the stressor.

What do I do if I suspect a child is being abused?

This will be discussed in more detail later, but just to make it clear at the outset, this chapter discusses the issues surrounding safeguarding children in a general way and provides broad guidance about policies and procedures. For the most recent government guides to your duty and the legislation that affects your role as someone who comes into contact with children and families with regard to safeguarding children, please see the additional guidance at the end of the chapter. Having said that, if you have any concerns about any children at this point you can *refer those concerns to children's social care or the police*. If you are in a setting or a school there will be procedures in place in your setting or school 'to be followed for reporting concerns about a particular child. This will normally be via the school's designated senior member of staff or their nominated deputy or if neither are available, another senior member of the school's staff. In emergencies, however, contact the police direct' (DfES, 2006: 10).

What constitutes abuse?

What constitutes abuse has been, historically, open to wide debate, in part because some researchers will state that what one group in society deems to be abuse, another will claim is a 'normal' part of child rearing practice. More general societal attitudes or dominant discourses will also change with regard to what is regarded as usual – or even desirable – practice (Corby, 2005: 79). For example, if we take some of the changing dominant discourses in British attitudes to child-rearing, there has been a change in attitude over the past 70 years from leaving small babies to cry and feeding them to a strict timetable, to that of seeking to comfort them when they cry and feeding them on demand. The dominant discourse with regard to smacking children continues to be somewhat ambivalent: while corporal punishment was banned in schools, children's homes and foster homes in 1987 (Poland banned it in 1783) the debate about families in Britain being able to use smacking as a method of punishment or correction, still rages. Interestingly, Britain is one of the few European countries not to have legislated against adults continuing to be allowed to hit children. Section 58 of the Children Act 2004 makes what is termed battery of a child illegal and battery illegal as a form of punishment; however, it does not per se make all forms of striking or hitting a child illegal. In Britain some forms of hitting children are still legal or, as it has been described in the press, 'mild smacking is legal but any blow which leaves a mark on a child is illegal' (Womack, 2006). In contrast with our immediate neighbours, this make Britain one of the last European Union (EU) countries where smacking is still legal. Sweden made the practice illegal in 1979, it is now illegal in Austria, Croatia, Cyprus, Denmark, Finland, Latvia and Norway and there is evidence that it has never be allowed in Greece, Italy and Luxembourg. However, In 1906 Britain did ban flogging in the army, but it was allowed in the Navy until 1957 and birching as a legal punishment for criminals came to an end in 1948 (Randall, 1998).

Physical injuries and abuse

The smacking debate is a good place to start in exploring where the delineation between what might be regarded as acceptable parenting practice and abuse starts and finishes. With practices such as smacking, which essentially involve hitting a child, there is the legally acceptable – and often culturally acceptable – smack that does not leave a lasting mark on a child, through a continuum of hitting that escalates to sustained hitting, beating with objects, punching, and so on, which is 'seriously abusive' (Corby, 2005: 85). The point at which any practice becomes abusive is the point at which it becomes ill-treatment, likely to impair health or physical, intellectual, emotional, social or behavioural development (DfES, 2006).

However, this is still not very helpful for a practitioner or other adult working with a child to know when reporting an incident or intervention might be necessary. The best advice would be to report anything that you feel concerned about. The guidance for how to do this is discussed later, but for general information the way decisions about whether what seems to be happening to the child is abuse or not will be based on issues such as the seriousness of the injury. Minor bruising, even if deliberately inflicted on a child, might not be deemed as seriously abusive if it seems to be a 'one-off' event; however, a series of unexplained bruises or injuries, particularly where investigation of the injury seems to uncover suspicious circumstances, is more likely to be pursued as abuse.

Another factor that will be considered when investigating an injury is that of intention. In terms of child protection agencies, while intentionality is crucial to making decisions about whether a child is at risk, it is understood that, at times children are unwittingly caught up, and sometimes accidentally injured, by other events. This is not to say that it would not be noted that if violence is routinely happening between others in the home that there is likely to be a harmful emotional impact on the child and that this itself would be a cause for considering the child to be at risk. Other factors that will be considered are the age of the child: generally the younger the child the greater the concern, as the younger the child the more vulnerable they are to concealment of any sustained abuse. As, for example, in the recent and terrible case of the death of 17 month-old 'Child P'. Other factors that will be investigated are if anyone has witnessed incidents that have led to the injuries (Corby, 2005: 87–9; Department of Health, 2005; DfES, 2006).

Activity

The whole area of child protection and safeguarding children can seem overwhelming, particularly if you come from an education rather than child protection background. It can make you feel quite anxious too to know that you have a responsibility to safeguard children, but not know what you are looking for or what to do if you are suspicious.

All settings and schools will have a policy about how that setting or school deals with these issues. The first thing to do is to find a copy of the policy – this is a very important aspect of practice, so if the policy is not obviously available, ask for it.

Once you have the policy go through it with the checklist below to hand.

continued

continued

- When was it last updated? The government regularly issues new guidance to settings and schools in this area, the policy should be reviewed as a matter of course every year, check on the Department for Children, Schools and Families website (www.dcsf.gov.uk) to see when the latest guidance was published – has the policy been updated to reflect the most recent guidance?
- Does the policy explain in a way you understand what constitutes abuse?
- Does the policy tell you what the most common and obvious signs of abuse are?
- If you suspect abuse does the policy tell you what to do?
- Having read the policy, do you feel more confident about safeguarding children? If the answer is no, do you know which member of staff to approach about these issues?
- All staffs will have at least one person designated to deal with safeguarding and child protection issues. If you are unsure who that is, ask your line manager.

Settings and schools need to provide regular training for their staff in this area, if you have not received any training and feel you would benefit from training, discuss this with your line manager.

Poisoning, suffocation and illnesses that are fabricated or induced

While these are rare forms of abuse, they are important to be aware of, particularly in cases of poisoning and illnesses that have been fabricated or induced (formally referred to as Munchausen's syndrome by proxy – Department of Health, 2005) as the harm and injuries from these forms of abuse can be happening to a child over a considerable period of time before the cause is properly detected. Parents or carers that fabricate or induce illness in children as making the child actually, or seemingly, unwell to gain attention for themselves. That is, because the child is unwell they will need specialist attention and in the wake of the child needing this attention the parent or carer will receive attention too. In such cases, although the child may be perfectly well, a parent, or carer suffering from the condition may administer substances to the child to make them unwell – often through poisoning them. Not only does the child suffer abuse through having the symptoms or illness induced in them, but from the resulting, sometimes unnecessary, medical treatment they are required to undergo, perhaps including surgery. This is a very complex area of abuse. If you have any concerns in this area you must seek further advice and information. There is also a Department for Health publication, *Safeguarding Children in Whom Illness Is Fabricated or Induced*, you can consult, the details of which are in the Further Reading list at the end of this chapter.

Physical neglect and failure to thrive

The definition of neglect is 'the persistent failure to meet a child's physical and/or psychological needs, likely to result in the serious impairment of the child's health or development' (DfES, 2006: 9) and it is often difficult to determine. Failure to thrive is often easier to determine than neglect, as it is often health agencies that pick up on children who are not developing physically along the expected continuum, and for whom there seems to be no medical reason that can be found for this failure to thrive. The harm and damage this form of abuse does to children can have devastating long-term consequences, since it will affect both physical and mental health. However, the causes of and the solutions to abuse through neglect and failure to thrive are complex, since they may be linked to poverty and other forms of material deprivation (Daniel, 2004). These issues are further explored in Chapter 8.

Sexual abuse

The DfES (2006) *What to Do if You Are Worried a Child Is Being Abused* document defines sexual abuse as:

> Sexual abuse involves forcing or enticing a child or young person to take part in sexual activities, including prostitution, whether or not the child is aware of what is happening. The activities may involve physical contact, including penetrative (e.g. rape, buggery or oral sex) or non-penetrative acts. They may include non-contact activities, such as involving children in looking at, or in the production of, sexual on-line images, watching sexual activities, or encouraging children to behave in sexually inappropriate ways. (DfES, 2006: 9)

Over the past 20 years it has been recognized that sexual abuse of children is more prevalent than had been previously thought to be the case. Sexual abuse affects children of all ages, all classes and all ethnicities. Sexual abuse goes undetected as children are coerced into not disclosing the abuse is taking place, through fear of what the perpetrator will do if the child does 'tell' or because the perpetrator is someone very close to the child and they are afraid of losing that person if they disclose the abuse. Young or very young children may be unaware that what is happening to them is wrong or not yet have the vocabulary or capacity to articulate what is happening. Sometimes it is the case that the partner of the abuser knows what is happening to the child but, even as a parent of that child, will allow the abuse to continue for fear of losing the emotional or financial support that they derive from the perpetrator.

Protecting children from the risk of sexual abuse

While there is considerable public concern about 'stranger danger' and children's risk of being 'snatched' and sexually assaulted, children are at greatest risk of being abused by people they know: '87 per cent of sexual assaults [are] committed by someone who is known to the child, such as a family member, neighbour or family friend' (ChildLine, 2003, in Sanderson, 2004). It is also much more likely that sexual abuse of this nature will be sustained and continue over a period of time, rather than be a 'one-off' event. That such close family members and friends can abuse children over a long period of time also indicates how capable abusers are at concealing their action from other adults around the child, and how effective they have been at ensuring the child is silent about the abuse.

The very real issue for all those who are concerned to protect children from sexual abuse is in knowing who is an abuser and how to enable the child to protect themselves. And since it is the abuser's intention to get close to children, it is also necessary that they are able to gain not only the trust of the child, but also of the adults around the child. For these reasons highly predatory child sexual abusers will make deliberate attempts to appear as normal as possible to allay any fears or suspicions that adults and children might have about them (NSPCC, 2005; Sanderson, 2004: 84). This makes the role of protecting children even more challenging. Paedophiles do not 'look' any different to those who have no desire to harm children, and since they will also work hard to appear as normal as possible, how can we know who to protect children from?

Random sexual assaults on children are rare, since it is not in the child sexual abuser's long-term interest to draw attention to their behaviour and risk being caught and imprisoned. Therefore, most paedophiles will adopt a far more successful and sustainable strategy to gain access to children known as 'grooming'.

What is 'grooming'?

As those responsible for the care and welfare of children have become more alert to the prevalence of child sexual abuse, one of the strategies paedophiles use to get close enough to children to be able to abuse them is what is known as 'grooming'.

Someone who is intent on sexually abusing a child knows that the adults around it will be on 'high alert' and is prepared to take considerable time and effort to win both the trust of the child and others. Indeed, that the paedophile takes the time and makes the effort to build the relationship contributes to the pressure the abuser can exert on the child to remain silent about the abuse. If the paedophile has become a family friend, or a trusted member of a group or community, they can use this as a lever to coerce the child into keeping silent.

Sexual grooming with the intent to sexually abuse children became a criminal offence under the Sexual Offences Act 2004 (Crown Prosecution Service, 2008) and an abuser found guilty of the crime can face up to 10 years' imprisonment.

Grooming takes place either through targeting the child's family, to get access to the child, or by approaching and befriending a child directly. Gaining the trust of the child occurs either through face-to-face encounters with the child, or, increasingly, via the Internet, in which the paedophile may pose as someone of the child's age.

Stages in the grooming process

A paedophile will select a specific victim, with a view to grooming the child with the intention of sexually abusing the child.

The paedophile will begin to engage the child and any adults around the child, very casually at first and then gradually build up the link over time. The paedophile will take time over this process and the unaware child or adult(s) will become victims of the grooming as they believe the paedophile simply wants to be their friend. The abuser may indeed groom the parents first, as a way to gain access to the child.

Once the relationship is established and on the face of it seems like any 'normal' relationship, the paedophile with then begin to engage the child in seemingly innocuous activities, ones that the abuser knows the adults around the child have forbidden – this might be something as simple as eating sweets before a meal or encouraging a child to say a 'naughty word'. By the very nature of the child the paedophile has chosen to groom, the abuser knows that they then have leverage over the child and can blackmail them with this information. 'I'm going to tell X what you did/said' or, 'I won't tell on you because I am your friend and it can be our secret'. Where a child is very trusting, or very careful not to transgress any rules set out by the adults around it, they will be susceptible to this form of coercion. While to adult ears this sounds very minor, to a child who has less life-experience and is used to doing what it is told, it will be genuinely very concerned not to be 'told on'. If the child goes along with keeping these events secret, then the paedophile will subtly escalate this behaviour to isolate the child from the adults around it and form a 'secret' relationship with the child.

When the paedophile has managed to establish this relationship with the child, they know it is now likely that they will be able to successfully manipulate the child to engage in sexual acts with them (NSPCC, 2005; Sanderson, 2004).

As Sanderson states: 'the grooming process is extremely subtle for both the parents and the child being groomed, with neither necessarily being aware of the hidden motives behind this process' (2004: 166). It is also likely that once the paedophile has broken down the child's resistance, 'the abuser [will reinterpret] the victim's behaviour as "she wanted it" or "he made me do it", which serves to justify the assault' (Sanderson, 2004: 91). However, as we have seen above, the law is very clear that no child can have assented to any form of sexual contact. The abuser may have said things to the child such as, telling them that it was their fault for encouraging the abuse, which is why it is essential that if a child discloses abuse, they must be reassured it is in no way their fault.

How do I know I or a child is being groomed?

Most adults who are involved in working with children, or are parents, however much they love being with children do also enjoy a break from them and want to enjoy time with their own peer group. Most adults are able to give themselves and children boundaries that separate out being an adult and pursuing their life as an adult and working with, or caring for, children. This is not to say the relationships between children and adults are not very close and very mutually rewarding. In being suspicious that you or a child is being groomed, one of the clues to look for is that the paedophile may behave in a way that is unusually child 'friendly', that they are not making that appropriate distinction between 'child-time' and knowing when it is normal to say 'enough', this is 'my time as an adult to be with my peers and do the things I like to do'.

Therefore, experts suggest that the signs that sexual grooming is happening are as given below:

- The paedophile may talk about children in ways that focus only on their 'innocence' or 'purity' or that they are 'lovely', or say things like: 'kids are great, I could spend all my time with kids', that there seems to be no understanding that children can also be demanding, trying, difficult and challenging.
- Abusers may be ultra knowledgeable about the latest childish crazes, films, television programmes, and so on, not only talking in unusual detail about them, but seeking to specifically have conversations with children about them, buying the 'spin-off' merchandising that goes with new children's films and, at some point inviting a child to come and see/play with their collection.
- They may use the 'latest' child-slang.
- They may seem to have the patience to play games with children beyond that which most adults have.
- They may offer to babysit and eventually take children for overnight outings or 'sleepovers'.
- They may treat a particular child as a favourite, making them feel 'special' by buying presents, or taking them on outings.
- They may have no close friends of their own age, or seek to engage in social activities with their own peers.
- Their homes may be decorated in a way that would appeal to a child, with evidence of childish activities around, games, books, DVDs, and so on.
- They will, at some point, manipulate the situation to allow them to spend time alone with a particular child (DfES, 2006; NSPCC, 2005; Sanderson, 2004).

Enabling children to protect themselves

In enabling children to protect themselves, all the guidance (DfEE, 2000; NSPCC, 2005; OfSTED, 2002) is very clear that the best way to enable children to protect themselves is:

- to educate them – in an age-appropriate way about sex and relationships, and from a young age;
- that the personal and social education aspects of the curriculum must be used to explore with children, what are wanted and unwanted behaviour in other people – people we like to hug and kiss, hugs and kisses we do not like, parts of the body that are 'special' to us and only we might touch;
- that children understand that they have the right to refuse any invitations from adults that are unwelcome;
- that there are good and bad secrets.

It is also important that all adults around the child seek to keep an honest and open relationship with them and are not prone to 'over-reacting' to questions asked by children, or children's minor transgressions of rules and behaviour. If a child does not feel that they can trust the adults around them and be confident that they will listen and respond in a caring way, they are less likely to express any fears they may have about things that are happening in their lives. For many settings and schools these are challenging areas to deal with in working with children, however, research shows (DfEE, 2000; OfSTED, 2002) that parents, too, find these issues challenging and many parents welcome support and advice from settings and schools about how to work together to tackle these issues.

Detecting sexual abuse is happening to a child

Unless a child discloses what is happening to them or, as is often the case in uncovering sexual abuse cases, is diagnosed with a sexual transmitted disease or becomes pregnant, it can be hard to know when a child is being sexually abused (DfES, 2006). Some behaviour indicators that may indicate sexual abuse, for example, particularly withdrawn children, children who's behaviour changes markedly, children who self-harm, or may even make an attempt on their own lives, running away from home and have anorexia nervosa have also been cited as indicators (DfES, 2006). Children may also: 'show unexpected fear or distrust of a particular adult, start using sexually explicit behaviour or language or describe receiving special attention from a particular adult, or refer to a new, "secret" friendship with an adult or young person' (NSPCC, 2008b).

Often the most reliable evidence that abuse has taken place comes from the child themselves, but again there is controversy over the reliability of children as witnesses, particularly where they may be talking about abuse perpetrated by a close family member – or even a parent. There are also concerns that a child having to recount distressing events is suffering further abuse at having to 're-live' the events.

If you suspect a child is being sexually abused, you must report it. If you do not know who to report it to in your local authority social care child protection team, report it to the police. If you are working in a setting or a school, you must report it to the designated member of staff who deals with abuse. They will take the issue from there and advise you what to do. If a child discloses to you that they are being sexually abused you have a *legal* duty to report any disclosures. If the disclosure happens while you are working with children in a setting or a school, you must explain to the child that you cannot keep secret anything they tell you. It is then your legal duty to inform the designated member of staff that a disclosure has been made. However, with regard to the child, the NSPCC's advice is to:

- keep calm;
- listen very carefully to what the child tells you;
- make clear that you believe what they are telling you;
- allow the child to tell you as much as they want to about the abuse, but do not force them to talk about it;
- tell the child that they have done the right thing in telling you;
- tell them that they are not to blame for the abuse (NSPCC, 2008b).

It is also advisable to make notes about what the child has told you as soon after the disclosure as possible.

Activity

Dealing with uncomfortable emotions

The section on sexual abuse may have generated many emotions in you. The important thing to remember here is that you are, or are training to be, a professional and as such you must make the welfare of the children you work with your priority.

You may have been sexually abused yourself as a child and reading this section may have made you feel angry or upset, confused or scared, particularly if you have never told anyone about what happened to you, or sought help to deal with the harm done to you. If this is the case, you will be better able to help the children you work with if you do find help for yourself. Many adults who experienced sexual abuse as children are still very confused about knowing where boundaries are and feel puzzled about their feelings about themselves, others and sex. Help and counselling for adults who have experienced sexual abuse is usually free and can be found in your local yellow pages or web pages that provide information about local services.

If talking about sex generally makes you feel uncomfortable, again you need to be able to separate out your personal feelings from your professional duty and what you are required to do. As a professional ensure you are familiar with the content of the personal, social and emotional aspect of the Early Years Foundation Stage framework, or the National Curriculum. Read carefully what the expectations are for children in terms of what they should know about sex and relationships, and at what age.

continued

continued

Find a copy of your setting or school policy for this area of the curriculum, find out what happens in this area of the curriculum for the children you work with and research resources available to help you explore these issues with children.

It may also be the case that you would benefit from some counselling to help you talk through why these issues make you feel so uncomfortable. This is not to say that 'you need therapy', but sometimes, often because of what they were told – or not told – as a child, adults have very ambivalent and confused feelings about sex. You may find it reassuring to talk through some of your thoughts and feelings with a counsellor.

Emotional abuse

Emotional abuse 'may involve conveying to children that they are worthless or unloved, inadequate, or valued only insofar as they meet the needs of another person'. It can also be caused by having expectations of children that are inappropriate for their age, either because they are 'beyond the child's developmental capability, as well as overprotection and limitation of exploration and learning, or preventing the child participating in normal social interaction' (DfES, 2006: 9). Emotional abuse can also occur where a child witnesses the ill-treatment of another, if for example, domestic violence is occurring in the home. Bullying, too is a form of emotional abuse, as 'Some level of emotional abuse is involved in all types of maltreatment of a child, though it may occur alone' (DfES, 2006: 9). Emotional abuse is particularly difficult to define; the difficulty is in agreeing where the line between where particular practices, usually parenting practices, move from being acceptable to unacceptable. For example, it can be challenging to know when a particularly authoritarian, or permissive, parenting style starts to be abuse. Corby suggests 'a child is suffering serious emotional damage, evidenced by severe anxiety, depression or withdrawal, or untoward aggressive behaviour or hostility towards others, and the parents are unwilling to provide treatment for the child' (Corby, 2005: 97).

What happens when I have passed on my concerns to social care, the police or the appropriate person in my setting or school?

Once you have discussed a concern about a child with the appropriate person in your setting or school, if they agree your concerns are serious they will:

• contact the relevant social care department of your local authority, following up their call in writing within 48 hours;

- on having the concern referred a course of action will be decided within one working day;
- where it is deemed necessary an initial assessment of the child's situation will be made, this must be completed within seven days of the referral; and
- the outcome of this will be either,
  - that the child is not likely to come to harm, but the family might benefit from some form of support;
  - emergency action may be necessary to safeguard the child; or
  - that a further enquiry, known as ans47 enquiry is instigated, which will be an in-depth assessment of the child's needs (DfES, 2006).

Personal, social and emotional education

We have seen in the previous chapter how there is considerable scope within the curriculum in the Early Years Foundation Stage framework and the National Curriculum for finding ways to raise the issues discussed with children – in a way that is age appropriate to them. The whole issue of raising children's awareness about their own safety is often most successfully dealt with through a multi-agency approach. Settings and schools have historically developed links with the police, particularly in asking police officers to come and talk bout 'stranger danger'. Now, in many areas it is the police community support officers (PCSOs) who undertake this work. The strength of making close links with the local PCSOs is that children will often see them in the local area, not only in the setting or school. Most PCSOs are very keen to get to know, and build relationships with, children and families in their area; they will come to the setting or school at different times of the day to help with traffic control around the buildings, cross children and families over busy roads and are a very good link into the community, beyond the remit of the setting or school.

Similarly, health-care workers are keen to work with other professionals and agencies, and will talk to practitioners, teachers and children about issues to do with sex education and drugs.

Supporting families

Many concerns about children that are referred result in the decision that the child is not in danger of immediate harm, but that the current circumstances of the family make the children vulnerable in the long term and that the family would benefit from support. Indeed, it has been a constant theme throughout this book that families that are helped to develop resilience and work through current problems can be the stronger for it. In the main, children suffer less long-term harm if they can remain with their families. Obviously where children are at risk of immediate harm this is not so – and local authorities, working with the police, have powers to remove children immediately where deemed necessary. To remove a child from its family is a decision that requires careful consideration, children love the people who are their family and want to be with them. Families are also the best placed units to care for their children, and removing children from a family can in itself cause long-term harm to the child and the well-being of the family. It is also recognized that relatives, particularly grandparents, can be a very good source of support since children can be fostered with grandparents, which will also allow them to have contact with their own parents, and indeed many families do set up their own support networks that include members of their extended family (Canavan, 2000: 20). This is not to say that some families do not have very severe problems which they need considerable support to deal with.

The support that can be offered to families varies depending on the family need. Sometimes where the family is very vulnerable and there are specific or multiple risks that, if not addressed, might cause long-tem harm to any children in the family, it is necessary, in the first instance, for social care workers to work with the family on a day-to-day basis. For example, where one or more parents may have a drug abuse problem children can be fostered on a daily basis. Some families will need to be put in contact with local groups and refuges offering support with specific issues, for example, support for families where there is domestic violence, child behaviour management programmes, support groups for children to help them deal with self-esteem issues – which might be the result of bullying or abuse. Other support strategies include assigning a key care worker to the family who will work alongside them, initially very intensively, to help establish routines in the home, ensure children are ready in time for school, have breakfast, do the washing, and so on. Most parents very much want to be 'good parents' and do the best for their children, but often we parent in the way that we were parented, since it is the model of parenting we have learnt. Therefore, adults whose own parenting was lacking, or who are very young parents, new to the area/country and very isolated, or may simply not know what to do, when given this kind of support will respond very well (Canavan, 2000: 15). This form of support is sometimes called *protective family support* and is successful because it recognizes the importance of the relationships within the family and builds on those strengths, helping establish 'routines (such as bedtime) and rituals (like birthdays and Christmas) in giving greater structure and stability to home life for a child in stressful family circumstances' (Canavan, 2000: 15).

Cultural factors to consider

One of the concerns with regard to safeguarding children that practitioners, teachers and others who work with children have is to know how do deal with cultural factors that affect different parenting practices. If we return to our discussion above about smacking, on the one hand, British law tells us what is deemed legal practice in this country, so any child that you may suspect of having been hit or beaten in a way that breaks the law must be referred. On the other hand, despite what the popular dominant discourse about the norm for some cultures to beat children would have us believe, it is not accepted in any culture (Corby, 2005: 80). Children are subject to physical abuse in all cultures, but not because it is a practice 'required' by that culture. It is because, for all the reasons we have explored in this chapter, some parents need support in finding alternative ways to discipline their children – or, for whatever other reasons, are abusing their children – and the children need to be safeguarded.

In terms of discussing cultural differences in child-rearing practices the dominant discourse will often fall back on examples of cultures where children are sent out to work – sometimes in the sex industry – young people are forced into arranged marriages, or girl's are denied education and have their personal freedoms severely restricted. This is not to say aspects of these practices do not constitute child abuse, but we are dealing with legal and acceptable levels of child safety in Britain. What we must first be clear about is, are we talking about these abuses when we find them happening in Britain or are we commenting on what is happening in another country? Although we cannot condone abuse of any child in any form, in terms of our responsibilities to the children we have a duty to safeguard in Britain, we are not comparing like with like if we compare what it is to bring up children in a comparatively rich, highly industrialized country like Britain with poor 'non-Western agrarian societies' where, through necessity children are 'economic assets' (Combrinck-Graham, 2006: 499). It is only since 1833 that Britain, against considerable opposition from employers and parents, began to legislate against children working, and initially it only applied to those aged under 9.

However, it cannot be ignored that the changing diverse cultural demographic of Britain does bring cultural tensions with it, and some of these tensions relate to perceived differences in childcare practices and perceptions of personal freedoms. Practitioners, teachers and others that work with children and families are often unsure of how to approach certain issues, particularly to do with gender equality tensions. Again, the law in Britain is very clear about what constitutes equality and entitlement to certain freedoms, and this is a useful starting place. It is also quite reasonable for you to have your own views on issues and for settings and schools to have policies pertaining to mutual respect between genders and what is deemed as suitable clothing. Where settings and schools have been successful in mitigating tensions between accepted practices in the setting and schools and expected norms by particular cultural groups, it is where the setting and schools have worked with the local community to discuss issues, understand the position of the other side and move forward with a common understanding. It is all about assumptions! 'Differentiating between culturally normative and abusive or neglectful parenting is a critically difficult but essential task for all practitioners involved in safeguarding children' (Corby, 2005: 81).

Case study 📁

Amina had recently arrived from Iraq with her husband and three small children of 5 years, 3 years and 18 months. She was a Muslim woman who wore a hijab and spoke little English. Amina and her family lived in a social housing flat on a large estate. She placed her eldest child in school and came to the local Children's Centre with her two younger children.

Some of the other mothers spoke to the Children's Centre staff saying that they were worried about the children as Amina seemed to be shouting at them a lot and had been seen to be pulling the 3-year-old along roughly.

Through approaching Amina and using the resources available to the centre, including the outreach community support worker and an interpreter, the centre was able to work with Amina and learn more about her. It transpired she felt very isolated, having left her family and home behind and moving to a country where she had no support networks to help her and no friends or family to turn to. She was also very concerned that people might think she could not control her children, that they were naughty and she would be thought a bad mother. The outreach worker was able to help the other mums in the area, who simply had not known how to approach Amina, to make contact with Amina and, over time, develop friendships.

Through attending toddler groups and staying with her children in the nursery Amina has become more confident in approaching others to chat and for help and advice, and those around her have realized that the hijab is not a barrier to approaching Amina. Indeed, as people got to know Amina they were keen to ask her questions about it and Amina was pleased to talk about her faith and culture, and dispel some of the myths that the press perpetuate about Islam. In the same way, she has been open to the help and advice that her new friends have given her to help her understand things about Britain.

Amina now has good friends in her new community, her children are settled and integrated into the community and she feels confident that she is a good mother and that others are there to support her.

Safeguarding from bullying and discrimination

Adults can often get it wrong when they decide what is bullying and what is not bullying (OfSTED, 2008a: 9). Settings and schools will often say 'we have no bullying here', their evidence being that the adults do not see it happening and the children do not report it to them. However, if children do not see their setting or school as being sympathetic to issues of bullying – that is, if they do not believe anything will be done about it – they will often fail to report it. And very young children may not know that what they are experiencing is bullying, and is wrong, or have the vocabulary to know how to tell an adult what is happening. Settings and schools need to be proactive in tackling bullying, and all forms of discrimination, and listen to what the children believe is happening – not what they think is the case.

The Office for Standards in Education has recently published its latest findings and guidance with regard to bullying. The report, *Children on Bullying: A Report by the Children's Rights Director for England* (OfSTED, 2008a), is particularly powerful as it is a report of research undertaken with children. The researchers held group discussions with 158 children and a further 161 filled in 'question cards'. The age of the children involved in the research ranged from 6 to a care leaver aged 20.

In discussing the issue with children, OfSTED states it is bullying if what is occurring is something that:

• a person feels is bullying, it is not necessarily a finite list of actions that can be defined as bullying;
• hurts someone who cannot defend themselves and does not deserve what happens to them;
• is unpleasant that is done to a child by a group of others and may be repeated;
• can be a mixture of physical violence and verbal hurting;
• children, like people in any group, will use to pull themselves up in the group by pushing others down – particularly individual, targeted others; and
• might be seen as joking, teasing, arguing, play fighting and name calling, but is not necessarily intended to be bullying (OfSTED, 2008a: 9).

In exploring with children where and when bullying occurs the children said that:

• it often happens at school, but those living in children's homes or residential schools also get bullied where they live;
• the street is a risky place for bullying;
• quiet places and being on your own can be risky;
• it can happen at most times of the day or night; and
• it is likely to happen where there is no staff supervision, including at break times (OfSTED, 2008a: 14–15).

In discussing with children who were most at risk of bullying, they said:

• anything that makes children different from others puts them at risk of being bullied;
• children who are seen as unable to stand up for themselves are at risk of being bullied;
• someone without friends around them risks being bullied;
• children who are part of a group or gang are safer from those in their own group, but more at risk from those in other groups; and
• children are better than adults at identifying who is likely to be bullied (OfSTED, 2008a: 18).

In discussing with children how to stop bullying, their answers were linked to the bullet points above, that is, if you are able to stand up for yourself and have friends to support you, you are less likely to be bullied. Overwhelmingly, children said the best protection from being bullied is to tell someone who will deal with the situation effectively. However, children also reported that adults could be very unpredictable in terms of what they would do when told about bullying. From a child's point of view the worst things adults might do is not believe that the bullying was happening or directly confront the bully, simply making the matter worse.

Cyber-bullying

With the increase in children's access to mobile telephones and the Internet, there has been a marked increase in what has become known as 'cyber-bullying'. Children in the primary school age range can be subject to this form of bullying, which includes embarrassing video clips, usually taken by mobile phone, which show children being hit or bullied, and which is then uploaded onto the public Internet websites. Children can be bullied through text messaging and through having bullying messages left on personal websites. There are policies and guidelines that website operators are bound to follow with regard to Internet bullying, and most are very responsive once they know what is happening.

Successful measures for combating bullying and discrimination

Bullying is dealt with well where:

- the setting or school works with the children to help them develop strategies for making friends;
- by working with all children to understand 'differences' – for example, that we are culturally different, physically different and may have different learning needs, religious backgrounds, and so on, often this work involves directly addressing those differences and talking about them;
- there are strategies to build self-confidence;
- there is access to a trained adult who deals with bullying;
- there is a known routine, or policy, so everyone knows what will happen if bullying is reported, which from the children's point of view should include:

  not getting anything out of proportion, not treating different bullying situations as the same and not taking action against the wrong person. It should also cover how to encourage children to believe that all are equal, how to create an anti-bullying atmosphere, and how to make bullies feel bad about being bullies. (OfSTED, 2008a: 41)

Peer mentoring

Many settings and schools have set up peer-mentoring schemes where older children are given some training in looking after and supporting younger children. Such schemes are particularly helpful for children who are going through a transition phase, perhaps from one age phase to another.

Further reading

Department of Health (2005) *Safeguarding Children in Whom Illness Is Fabricated or Induced*. London: Department of Health: www.dh.gov.uk/en/Publicationsandstatistics/Publications/PublicationsPolicyAndGuidance/DH_4008714

HM Government (2006) *Working Together to Safeguard Children: A Guide to Inter-Agency Working to Safeguard and Promote the Welfare of Children*. London: TSO.

Office for Standards in Education (OfSTED) (2008a) *Children on Bullying: A Report by the Children's Rights Director for England*. London: HMI.

Useful websites

www.everychildmatters.gov.uk/workingtogether/

Beat bullying: www.bbclic.com/

Don't suffer in silence: www.dcsf.gov.uk/bullying/parentsandindex.shtml

www.kidscape.org.uk/

6

Enjoying and Achieving

This chapter explores:

- different models of children's learning;
- what is meant by personalized learning and how it can enable children to enjoy and achieve;
- how Assessment for Learning (AfL) can enable children to enjoy and achieve; and
- good practice in developing relationships between Early Years settings, schools and home, and how to build on the good practice developed in this area in Children's Centres.

To meet the Every Child Matters Outcomes Framework (DCSF, 2008b) for the third element of the Every Child Matters agenda – that of enjoying and achieving – Early Years settings and primary schools need to demonstrate that they enable children to be ready for learning, that children enjoy their learning and achieve stretching educational standards.

From the point of view of Early Years settings and primary schools, enabling children to enjoy their learning and to achieve their learning potential is at the heart of their work. While settings and schools are also very involved in ensuring children are healthy, safe, make a positive contribution and enjoy economic well-being, and that children achieve these goals both in the short term and as long-term outcomes, enabling children to learn is, for settings and schools, their area of expertise. Settings and schools are also the places that can bring together all the elements children and families need to help them achieve the ECM outcomes. Settings and schools have the opportunity to help children learn about being healthy, safe and making a positive contribution, since they are places where children can develop lifelong skills, knowledge and understanding about how to make these outcomes happen for themselves in the long term. They are also places where if children enjoy and achieve in their learning, they will go on to achieve their own economic well-being. Settings and schools have a further important role to play in the wider community in that they are also places where families and other support agencies can come together to make contact with each other and ensure any necessary wider support needed by the child or family can be accessed.

There is a wealth of research that underlines the importance of children needing a positive experience of learning in the Early Years and at primary school, and how the quality of that experience will impact on a child's later educational achievement and eventual economic well-being. Children who do not enjoy and achieve in their learning may, at some point, cease to engage with the learning process. Where children are no longer motivated to want to learn this can, in the short term lead to disruptive behaviour, even exclusion, and in the long-term will impact on their likelihood of achieving qualifications, engagement in lifelong learning and possibly on their capacity to achieve economic well-being.

While being experts in terms of children's learning in the setting or classroom, settings and schools are also very aware that for a child to enjoy their learning and achieve in learning terms there needs to be mutually respectful and supportive relationships between the child's home and the setting or school. Indeed, in discussing the principles of personalized learning the DCSF (2008a) recognize that what they call 'beyond the classroom' has a significant part to play in enabling children to enjoy and achieve. It is recognized that settings and schools are in a good position to make links for children and families with other agencies that could also provide necessary support for vulnerable children and families. In this respect, sometimes the setting or school will be the first agency that recognizes that the child or family needs support. In this way the setting or school is in a good position to be *a broker* or *an advocate* for vulnerable children and families who might not know where to go for help or have the necessary skills to be able to seek help (DCSF, 2008a). In the same way, where settings and schools can also benefit children, in the wider sense, to enjoy and achieve is through the effective pastoral care they can offer and the capacity to 'spot' and tackle any learning needs children may have, referring children to specialist support where necessary. In Chapter 8 we explore in more detail how the provision of extended services and community partnerships can benefit the child and whole family in this way. However, what is at the heart of the term 'beyond the classroom' is the importance of the quality of the relationship the setting or school has with the child's home and family, as this will be a huge determiner in how the child enjoys and achieves in their learning since settings, schools and 'government do not bring up children – parents do' (DCSF, 2007d: 4).

Much has been written to support those who are engaged in delivering learning activities for children and that provides ideas and support in designing engaging learning activities. For this reason, this chapter explores features of the enjoy and achieve aspect of the ECM agenda that are still new to many settings and schools, and in terms of approaches to helping children enjoy and achieve in their learning, which are less well developed than many other educational practices. The aspects of learning this chapter focuses on are personalized learning and Assessment for Learning. A further reason for this focus is that, in keeping with the notion of social justice, these are approaches to learning that involve the child in the design and planning of their own learning experience, rather than simply having the learning 'done to them'.

What is learning about anyway?

It is generally accepted that there are two beliefs held about how the process of learning can take place:

1. The transmission model – this is that knowledge can be transmitted to and learnt by another, and that fully understanding the content of that knowledge, including how to apply it, will come at some point, but is not essential to learning at this point.
2. The interactive model – where the learner is directly engaged in their own learning, possibly through the planning and management of aspects of it.

Therefore, when we come to plan, design and deliver learning activities, we will either be focused on simply getting across specific knowledge and understanding, or we will be concerned about how the children we work with learn and how best we can design activities that they will engage with and then learn through that engagement. In most settings and primary schools the transmission model of learning has, to a greater extent, been superseded by the interactive model of learning and indeed this is reflected by the curriculum documentation itself, particularly in the Early Years. The inclusion agenda and the understanding that different children have different styles of learning (Knowles, 2006) have also contributed to our skills, knowledge and understanding in planning and delivering learning activities that enable children to enjoy and achieve in terms of their learning.

It is not only our beliefs about how children learn that affect children's achievement, a child's achievement will also be affected by what we believe the learning potential and capacity of any given child might be (Black and Williams, 2001: 9). For many years the notion that children possess an innate 'level' of intelligence dictated the learning experience of most of the school population. Children were tested to find their intelligence quotient (IQ) which was seen as being fixed from birth and, depending on how high or low their score, this would either enhance or restrict a child's capacity to learn and achieve and, therefore, they would be taught according to this expectation.

Most people who work with children in any capacity in a learning environment will quickly reject the notion that children have a fixed level of intelligence. While some children will struggle more than others to take on board some of the skills, knowledge and understanding presented in learning activities, there are very few children who cannot be engaged and motivated to progress in their learning and often to achieve in ways that might not have been previously expected. This way of approaching learning is what Black and Williams (2001) call the 'untapped potential theory': 'Here, the underlying belief is that all pupils can learn more effectively if one can clear away, by sensitive handling, the obstacles set up by previous difficulties, be they of cognitive failures never diagnosed, or of damage to personal confidence, or a combination of the two' (Black and Williams, 2001: 9).

The next two sections of this chapter supports the 'untapped potential' theory of learning and looks at how concepts of personalized learning and Assessment for Learning can support children's enjoyment in, and achievement of, learning.

The principles at the heart of personalized learning

Settings and schools have been working hard over the past few years to ensure they provide an inclusive learning environment for children, meeting all aspects of children's learning needs, be they those influenced by factors related to the child's age, gender, ethnicity, talents, gifts; or to a more specific learning need occasioned by a special educational need or disability. Settings and schools are also very good at considering a range of learning styles through which children may prefer to access their learning, routinely providing access to learning via learning activities that can be accessed through a visual, auditory or kinaesthetic style (Knowles, 2006). The achievement children are making in their learning is also reflected in the continuing rise in the number of children achieving the required standards and above in the National Curriculum tasks and tests, particularly in English and mathematics (OfSTED, 2008e: 7). Given the work practitioners, teachers and others have put into this aspect of children's well-being, it is hard to know what else can be done to help children achieve. However, while settings and schools have done much to look at broad aspects of how they provide for and support learning, where personalized learning can further benefit children's achievement is in terms of working with the child to involve them in the learning process, so their learning is a partnership with the setting or school, rather than something that is 'done to them', however sensitive and sympathetic to their needs.

The DCSF's introduction to personalized learning endorses the untapped potential approach to learning, stating: 'we must begin by acknowledging that giving every single child the chance to achieve their full potential, whatever their talent or background, is not the betrayal of excellence, it is the fulfilment of it' (DCSF, 2008a). They further describe a personalized learning approach as one which will:

- involve children as *joint partners* in the design of their learning;
- meet children's learning needs in and beyond the school environment;
- provide additional support for children who are not fulfilling their predicted potential; and

- enable children to respect others and their learning needs and develop their own self-esteem thorough learning in a mutually supportive environment (DCSF, 2008a).

Involving children as joint partners in the design of their learning

In terms of planning their learning activities, settings and schools have a number of external influences that impact on what learning experiences they provide for children. Both phases of education have their own curriculum documents that they must, by law, ensure they are using to plan the curriculum from. For Early Years settings this is the Early Years Foundation Stage framework (EYFS) and for primary schools they ensure they are meeting the demands of the National Curriculum for Key Stages 1 and 2. Further to this, primary schools are also provided with guidance in their literacy and numeracy planning and teaching through the Primary National Strategy. Settings and schools are also inspected by OfSTED and are mindful that the standards of achievement their children attain throughout their time in the setting or school will reflect on how the setting or school is perceived by others. While the EYFS and NC approach managing the discrete subjects within the curriculum in different ways, settings and schools can feel there is a tension between providing the full range of curriculum entitlement outlined in the documents and ensuring they tailor-make their provision to the learning needs of individual children, particularly where the DCSF states that 'personalised learning means high quality teaching that is responsive to the different ways students achieve their best' (DCSF, 2008a). In exploring how to begin to reconcile these tensions let us look at the requirements of the EYFS and the NC and examples of where settings and schools have been successful in personalizing learning for children.

Learning in the Early Years

The *Statutory Framework for the Early Years Foundation Stage* (DfES, 2007a) sets out as one of the main principles underpinning learning in the Early Years as being about: 'Laying a secure foundation for future learning through learning and development that is planned around the individual needs and interests of the child' (DfES, 2007a: 7) and it recognizes the uniqueness of every child. In terms of learning and development, the EYFS states that children should by the age of 5 have acquired the knowledge, skills and understanding embedded in the six early learning goals, which are:

1. personal, social and emotional development;
2. communication, language and literacy;
3. problem-solving, reasoning and numeracy;
4. knowledge and understanding of the world;

5. physical development; and
6. creative development (DfES, 2007a: 11).

While the DfES (2007a) provides guidance as to what children should cover in each early learning goal, and should have achieved in terms of skills, knowledge and understanding by the age of 5, it does not stipulate to settings how they should actually plan and 'set out' specific learning activities for children. In this way, settings have considerable freedom in how they plan and manage the learning environment and most settings will work in a thematic way, that is, deciding on learning themes they are going to cover across the year, then breaking that down in to more medium-term planning – that is, what they want to have as their themes across a few weeks and then into short-term planning, looking at what they want to cover over a week or two weeks. Once specific themes have been identified and how long they will run for, it is possible to map the different elements of the early learning goals against the themes, to ensure they are being covered. Most settings will then organize their staff and resources so staff will be responsible for the setting up of particular aspects of the early learning goals and related learning activities. This will include ensuring that the 'messy' play area, the wet play area and the outdoor activity areas have activities that link with the themes and the chosen aspects of the early learning goals. Most settings have also adopted a key-worker system, so particular adults are responsible for specific children and in this way can monitor their engagement in activities, their learning progress and ensure that the children's individual needs and interests are being met.

In terms of personalized learning – building on children's interests and developing their learning – the adults in the setting will work and play alongside the children, engaging the children in 'discussion by asking open-ended questions like 'I wonder why … ?'; 'I wonder what happens when … ?'; 'How do you think you will … ?'; and waiting for the children to think about their reply' (OfSTED, 2007a: 12).

Case study 📁

The children in Little Monkeys nursery in the West Midlands had been working on the theme of people who help us. They had been talking about hospitals and some of the children were particularly interested in hospitals. Following on from this, in the outside play area a group of children, with their key worker, were playing on some of the tricycles saying they were ambulances. One of the children said she had hurt her leg and needed to be taken to the hospital by ambulance. The key worker asked the children: 'How would the hospital know that they had to send an ambulance?' The children thought about this and after further talking about the situation, and the key worker prompting their thinking and problem-solving with more questions, the children developed one part of the play area as the ambulance station and another part of the area as the accident and emergency (A&E) unit. Two children

continued

continued

sat in the 'ambulances' waiting to be called, while another child acted as a receptionist taking the emergency calls and other children were doctors and nurses receiving the injured child.

In all, it took a morning for the children to develop their ideas to this level. Through the input of the key worker, who asked the necessary questions, and moved the children on in their thinking, the children covered aspects from all six of the early learning goals, personalized to their learning needs and interest in the theme being explored. For example, with regard to communication, language and literacy, children would used Post-it notes and made written marks – depending on where they were in terms of their own literacy – to record telephone and other messages that needed to be passed between the ambulance station and the doctors and nurses in the A&E unit.

Other examples of how learning can be personalized for children in the Early Years can be through letting children choose, from the activities available, those they wish to do – or the order in which they do them. Some settings will also expect children to 'take care of their environment and to choose or prepare their own snacks' or contribute to their planning for learning by making mind-maps of what they already know about a new topic or theme, and what they want to find out (OfSTED, 2008b: 14). In this way, learning is personalized since:

> Adults are able to adapt activities in response to children's individual needs, and spontaneously take advantage of everyday experiences. This enlivens children's curiosity and maintains their enthusiasm so that they participate eagerly throughout the session, extending their skills and understanding further. (OfSTED, 2008b: 13)

The National Curriculum

Where the EYFS early learning goals are organized into areas of learning, the learning in the NC is structured by more traditional subject headings, so in the NC there are the core subjects of English, mathematics and science and the foundation subjects of design and technology, information and communication technology, history, geography, art and design, music and physical education. After the introduction of the NC, which came about with the Education Act 1988, many schools moved away from a topic- or thematic-based approach to the curriculum to a subject-based approach. However, as schools have become more confident in the quality of their provision, supported by national statistics that show children's standards of attainment are rising, many are adopting a more thematic approach to delivering the curriculum. The advantages of the topic or thematic approach are that schools can develop a more creative curriculum, where natural links between subjects are made, which supports children's learning and allows for a more personalized learning approach to be adopted. While the DCSF endorse personalized learning as a way to enable children to enjoy and achieve in school, they make no stipulations about how a personalized learning programme should be implemented in a school, or indeed what it should look like. Indeed, they recognize that it will look different in different schools since what a school does will be determined, in part, by how it deploys its resources and staff.

Where schools have developed a personalized learning approach, it has been in those schools that recognize the benefits to pupils of teaching to their learning styles and of the importance of creativity in the curriculum. 'In these schools, teachers encourage pupils to become independent learners and involve them in assessing their own progress' (OfSTED, 2005e: 22). Other schools have adopted a more partial approach to personalized learning, using it more in the non-core subject areas, where foundation subjects can be taught in a cross-curricular way through a topic or thematic approach. Again, where it is used effectively to help children enjoy and achieve it is where children are involved in planning the curriculum and pursuing areas in the topic that interest them. In this way, the learning focus is on what is to be learnt and how that can best be achieved and the curriculum can be used to 'support a set of skills rather than as an end in itself, matching the aims of the National Curriculum to the areas of' the child's 'learning profile' and 'using ICT to help pupils manage their own learning, such as through a virtual learning environment whereby pupils can communicate with staff more freely' (DCSF, 2008a).

Case study

In a Year 5 class in a Somerset junior school the topic for the half-term was the Second World War. The teacher provided the children with an outline of the areas she wanted to cover in the topic and the aspects of the history and geography National Curriculum programmes of study that also needed to be covered.

The children discussed what they already knew about the Second World War, areas of the topic that specifically interested them and how they might use the elements of the programmes of study that needed addressing to structure a framework personalized to their own interests.

The children made maps of places central to that period of history; they made models of the clothes worn at the time and the air-raid shelters built. They also produced posters and information leaflets on other aspects of the Second World War and designed quizzes and gave three-minute PowerPoint presentations to each other, to ensure all children had accessed all aspects of the history and geography programme of study knowledge and understanding that needed to be covered. Approaching the topic in this way also involved children in developing and refining their research skills and independent learning skills, as well as appreciating the need to plan, set targets and review progress.

In exploring these approaches to learning, those adults involved in structuring the learning environment may feel concerned about their role in the learning process and worried about how they can know children are making necessary and appropriate progress in their learning. Personalizing learning in this way does not make teachers and support assistants redundant, it simply requires schools to think about how best to deploy staff to ensure learning is taking place. It is still necessary for teachers and others to know what skills, knowledge and understanding are needed to be learnt in a topic and to monitor individuals to ensure appropriate learning is taking place, but what is also needed – as seen in the discussion of personalized learning in the Early Years (above) – are adults working alongside children, asking the right questions to move them on in their learning and to ensure learning opportunities are not missed. In this way, the DCSF state that two very important features of personalized learning are:

- that schools will need to ensure they are using the support of 'non-teaching staff and other adults from outside the school to provide a holistic, tailored educational provision for all their pupils'; and
- that schools 'will seek to configure their design, resources, curriculum and organisation around the needs of their learners, to reflect a professional ethos that accepts and assumes every child comes to the classroom with a different knowledge base and skill set, as well as varying aptitudes and aspirations' (DCSF, 2008a).

Organizing the school

Where settings and schools are successful in adopting a personalized learning approach to enjoying and achieving, is where they have considered features of the process that impact on the whole setting or school (DCSF, 2008a). For example, for personalized learning to impact positively on children's learning achievement and enjoyment the following systems need to be in place:

- Children need time to talk to adults about what they have learnt, what they have enjoyed and what interests them, to set and review targets – and parents too need to be involved in this process.
- The setting or school needs to canvass the views of children and parents on the effectiveness of the learning experience – and be prepared to respond to what is being said.
- There needs to be a commitment, by the setting or school, to involving children and parents in contributing to the wider work of the setting or school.
- Settings and schools are focused around the needs of the children, rather than the adults in the setting or school, or existing systems of delivering provision.
- The setting or school has a well developed inclusion ethos and is an environment where children feel secure and can flourish as individuals; and there are clear sanctions combined with praise, for all children.
- Settings and schools celebrate and promote children's achievement (DCSF, 2008a).

Assessment for Learning

In its discussion of the principles that underpin personalized learning the DCSF sees effective teaching and learning and Assessment for Learning as central to a successful setting or school personalized learning policy (DCSF, 2008a). To a greater extent what might constitute an effective teaching and learning approach to personalized learning has been explored in the previous section and throughout the discussion, the notion of ensuring that learning progress was being monitored was a recurring theme (Black and William, 2001); it is for this reason that for personalized learning to ensure enjoyment and achievement in learning, it must go hand-in-hand with Assessment for Learning. That is, for personalized learning to be successful, it must include strategies that:

- make use of assessment data for each child, which is used to inform teaching and learning; and
- the policy will make provision for 'every young person's needs to be assessed and their talents developed through a variety of teaching strategies' (DCSF, 2008a).

Further to this, in terms of Assessment for Learning, the children themselves will be involved in monitoring their own achievement by being involved in the assessment process.

Assessment is central to successful learning. It is most successful where outcomes from assessments are used to plan the next stages in a child's learning and where feedback that results from an assessment being made can be acted on by the learner, or the teacher, to inform the next step in the learning process to reflect on what might be a more suitable teaching strategy, since 'frequent assessment feedback helps attainment' (Black and Williams, 2001: 3).

In exploring personalized learning we have seen how effective learning is about engaging children in problem-solving and thinking ideas through. It is not necessarily always about having a product – for example, a piece of writing – or marks on paper, at the end of the learning activity. Learning is not always measured by how much a child 'has produced' and how neatly they have presented their endeavour; indeed, focusing on these aspects of 'production' can often stultify the learning process. Similarly, adults can also be overly concerned with marking and grading work, rather than helping the child with what precisely is to be learnt and providing the activity in a way the child can access it. Poor use of assessment feedback, which emphasizes what the child has done incorrectly – or 'got wrong' – teaches children only what they cannot do, not what they have learnt and, particularly for children who struggle to achieve, it can lead to the belief that they cannot learn (Black and Williams, 2001: 4). Further to this, in terms of using assessment as a learning tool, there can also be an overemphasis on the managerial role of assessment, that is, on keeping records to show that learning has been assessed, rather than on determining the learning needs of the children and using this information to plan better for those needs (Black and Williams, 2001).

The importance of formative assessment

Generally the assessments we make fall into a range of categories. The two most often used are explored below.

Summative assessment

These are the overall judgements we make about what has been achieved in a learning activity. These can be made in the short term – for example: a tick at the end of a piece of work; or a comment such as 'well-done'; or 'try harder – spelling and punctuation need correction'; or we might give a grade, a star, house point, mark out of 10, National Curriculum level 2a, 5b, and so on. Summative assessments can also be made after a period of time has passed to make an overall judgement about a child's progress in the medium or long term. For example, many schools will ask children to undertake a particular piece of work every half-term, which is then given a National Curriculum level, to help determine how the child is progressing overall in any given subject. The levels children achieve at the end of key stages, through their NC tasks and test are summative assessments. The level they are given at the end of the key stage makes a summative judgement of what they have attained at that point.

Formative assessment

Summative assessments are very useful for determining achievement over a period of time, but to really help the learner understand what they are doing well and what they need to be 'working on', feedback on their learning and achievement in the short term, or formative assessment, is the most helpful form of ongoing assessment for children. Most of us when we are working with children do give feedback – or formative assessment – all the time, throughout the day. To ensure it is as effective as it can be for children, we need to ensure that the formative assessment we use follows the ideas given below:

- Before the child begins the learning activity they know exactly what is expected of them – that is, what the learning is about, sometimes called intended learning outcomes (ILOs), what we are learning today (WALT) or what I am looking for (WILF).
- We need to ensure that the ongoing comments we make to the child throughout the learning activity focuses on how they are demonstrating their learning in relation to what they have been asked to do. For example, if we wanted them to know the differences between canine and molar teeth and the different functions they perform, our comments should be in relation to these learning outcomes, we do not need, in this instance, to comment on spelling and punctuation. Similarly, in a learning activity where we may want children to learn about the purpose of full stops, we would not need to comment on the creative narrative content.

Activity

The concept of Assessment for Learning builds on the work of Black and Williams (2001) and Black (2003). The discussion from their research in this area shows that good feedback is essential to help children know what they have done well in terms of their learning and what they need to do next.

The next time you work with children on a learning activity, use the checklist below to help you ensure you are providing the support and helping the children to get the most from the activity:

- Are both you and the children completely sure what the learning intentions are for this activity?
- Have you explained them to the children, written them somewhere they can see them so they can refer to them throughout the activity – or presented them in a pictorial form – so they know what they are?
- Have you checked with the children that they understand them?
- Have you talked through with the children what the success criteria for the achievement of the learning intentions are?
- As you and the children work through the activity, do you give frequent feedback that is directly related to the learning intentions. For example, you could say things like: 'I think the way you have done X is good and meets Y success criteria, but I see you are struggling with B. What can we do to improve in that area?'
- Where there are a lot of children engaged in one activity, do you make provision for them to work with buddies so they can give feedback to each other and help each other achieve against the success criteria?
- At the end of the activity do you and the children have a general evaluation of what went well (WWW), and agree any revision that is needed or talk about the next steps in that aspect of the learning?

The person who should stand to gain most from assessment information is the child, since it is there to assess what has been learnt and to plan the next steps in the learning process for that child. This means not only what is to be learnt, but how the task is presented and how the child might access the task and in what form demonstrate their learning. Where the task is a narrowly designed activity whose outcome is only measured in terms of arriving at particular 'correct' answers, which can only be demonstrated through a written form, well presented, then this immediately narrows the child's learning to working towards the 'correct' answer, rather than exploring or taking risks with ideas. If the child also struggles with writing and presentation, then there will come a point where the child will not even bother to start. Where learning outcomes can only be achieved in these ways Black and Williams (2001) report that where there is any choice in the tasks, children will seek to avoid those that seem 'difficult' and will not take risks and be experimental.

What does work for children is that they have clearly defined feedback in response to particular aspects of their learning, that they are not directly, or indirectly, compared to others and that any messages the adult working with them gives is 'not clouded by overtones about ability, competition and comparison with others' (Black and Williams, 2001: 6).

EYFS and NC assessment requirements

Monitoring and assessment in the Early Years

In the Early Years, the early learning goals for each of the six areas of learning set out what a child should have achieved by the age of 5. At the end of the Foundation Stage the child's achievement against the early learning goals will be recorded in the child's Early Years Foundation Stage profile by those working with the child. Ideally, the EYFS profile will not only record the child's progress towards meeting the early learning goals, but will also provide useful information for the child's Year 1 teacher to help them plan an appropriate curriculum for the child as they enter Key Stage 1 (DfES, 2007b: 12). Again, there are no hard and fast rules about how and when information about a child's progress should be recorded, but many settings use practice that includes 'photographs, notes from observations, narrative records of discussions and conversations, together with parents' and children's contributions' (OfSTED, 2007b: 24). It is also recognized good practice that the information in the EYFS profile is shared with children and their families as well as being passed on to the child's school, since the profile reflects the learning achievement of the child, as well as the aspects of the early learning goals that have been attained (OfSTED, 2007a: 12; 2007b: 24).

Monitoring progress in the National Curriculum

Each of the subjects in the NC has its own level descriptors. For children in Key Stage 1 (ages 5–7) it is expected that children will achieve level 2 in all subjects by the end of Key Stage 1, while for children in Key Stage 2 (ages 8–11), it is expected that they will achieve level 4 in all subjects by the end of Key Stage 2. This is not to say that some children achieve above, or below, level 2 at the end of Key Stage 1 and above, or below, level 4 at the end of Key Stage 2. In practice most primary schools concentrate on tracking children's progress against the NC levels mainly in terms of English, mathematics and science. At the end of each key stage a formal assessment in English, mathematics and science is made, either through teacher assessment or NC tests, the outcomes of which are public and are used to draw up the school 'league tables'.

Self-assessment

For learning to be enjoyable and to allow children to demonstrate appropriate achievement in their research Black and Williams (2001) also found that children are more motivated to learn and achieve more in their learning when they are allowed to be responsible for aspects of their learning. This may be as in the case study above, where children have some choice or control over how the 'finished product' might be produced. That is, it is the learning that is important, so the child might record what they have learnt in the form of a model, a poster, a presentation or, because some children enjoy writing, a more traditional piece of written work. Obviously where it is writing that is being learnt about, the product will be writing, but there are many genres of writing and the genre being taught needs to be linked to a real purpose and audience. For example, if the children are learning about report writing, they might write a report of a football game they played in at the weekend or of a television programme they watched. Similarly, if you are teaching about writing lists, this can be done as an activity in the role-play area, where, for example, you are doing a topic about journeys and you want the children to write a list of clothes they would need to pack for a journey to a cold country.

In terms of exploring how assessment helps children enjoy and achieve in their learning we have considered assessment only so far as adults are the ones making the assessments. Where Assessment for Learning can make most impact in enabling children to achieve in their learning is where children are involved in self-assessment, that is, in being able to make their own, informed judgements against success criteria about what they have achieved. To engage children in this process, particularly if it is new to them, will require some time and effort, and for it to make an impact on the children's learning the learning activity will need to be motivating and interesting for the child.

What does AfL look like?

Where a setting or school encourages use of an AfL approach to monitoring and assessment of children's learning, the following elements of good practice will be in place.

- All learning activities will be organized in a way that ensures all children can achieve in them.
- Any assessments made will provide helpful evidence of learning for both the adult and the child.
- Everyone knows what their target in any given learning activity is – these may be individual, small group or whole class/large group targets and may be framed as learning intentions.
- Any assessments, or measurements of achievement, are made in relation to what is valuable in the learning process.

During the learning activity and at the end of the activity the child will be provided with:

continued

continued

- continuous oral/written feedback which identifies strengths and the next step for improvement;
- encouraged to use self-assessment strategies;
- opportunities for all pupils to demonstrate their achievements in their first language;
- questioning that promotes learning and problem-solving and allows time for children to think through their answer, rather than expecting an instant response; and
- time for focused observation of teacher-directed and child-initiated activity (Black and Williams, 2001; QCA, 2008).

In discussing what constitutes AfL the Qualifications and Assessment Authority (QCA) outline 10 principles that underpin the process, the two of which we have already explored that are:

- Assessment for Learning should be part of effective planning of teaching and learning; and
- Assessment for Learning should focus on how students learn.

The QCA also recognize that for AfL to be a successful tool in enabling children to achieve: it needs to be central to classroom practice and not simply a 'bolt-on'; how it is used with children must reflect that being assessed, even assessing oneself, can have an emotional impact; the learners' motivation will impact on their success with the learning activity; for children to be able to assess their achievement they must understand the assessment, or success criteria, for the learning activity; and learners must receive constructive guidance about how to improve (QCA, 2008). That is:

- children must be engaged in a dialogue with adults to establish what the learning intentions for the given activity are and what the success criteria for reaching those intentions will look like;
- there must be dialogue throughout the learning activity, between the learner and the adults and between learners – including formative feedback against the success criteria to help the learner meet the learning intention; and
- it must be recognized by all involved that the learner's self-esteem can be as easily damaged through this process as it can be significantly enhanced (Black and Williams, 2001: 8; QCA, 2008).

With regard to AfL, OfSTED have commented that where it is working well to support enjoyment and achievement is where 'teachers are improving their assessment techniques, questioning is targeted effectively, pupils are encouraged to discuss and comment on their learning, and success criteria are used to help pupils evaluate learning outcomes' (OfSTED, 2005e: 7).

Activity

Where a setting or school encourages use of an AfL approach to learning the following elements of good practice will be in place. Learning activities are constructed to ensure that:

- questioning techniques that prompt thinking about the learning activity and how it relates to previous learning are used, including questions that begin: 'how could we ... ?', 'what could we ... ';
- techniques such as modelling, and scaffolding of learning are used;
- there is a shared involvement in and construction of activity;
- there is range of activities that can be used to explore the learning, including guided tasks, opportunities for independent working, collaborative working and partnerships; and
- children have the opportunity to reflect, draft and re-draft, explore, revisit learning and ideas, talk ideas through and design their own tasks.

If you have access to an assessment policy, or where you are working in a setting or school, note the elements of good practice you see.

Where AfL practices are working well the research of Black and Williams (2001) showed that one of the strengths for the learner is that they begin to understand the whole of the learning process, rather than experiencing individual learning activities in a fragmented way. They understand where the learning activities are taking them and by being engaged in assessing their own achievement they can monitor, for themselves, their success in the process and, where necessary, know when they are struggling and would benefit from more support or for concepts to be explained again or further practice in a particular aspect undertaken.

Beyond the classroom – engaging families and children from birth

With the inception of the Children's Centres it is now much easier to reach out to parents and begin working with them to build partnerships that will sustain the child in achieving the five ECM outcomes, even before the children are born. Most Children's Centres have some form of outreach worker who can make contact with those who are about to be parents as well as new and established parents. Indeed, many Children's Centres will be the place that pregnant women are initially referred to for ante-natal care and from this point can then 'tap in' to all the services for both themselves and their child or children that the centre offers, be that health care, day care, pre-school provision, aerobics and yoga classes, toddlers groups, fathers' groups, and many other services besides. The Office for Standards in Education (2008b) recognizes and applauds as an example of good practice the outreach work done by Children's Centres to make those initial links and relationships with parents and families. The same OfSTED report also acknowledges the good practice achieved by outreach workers in making links with particularly 'hard-to-reach' or vulnerable children and families, including:

- teenage mothers and pregnant teenagers;
- lone parents;
- children in workless households;
- children in Black and Minority Ethnic groups;
- disabled children and children of disabled parents; and
- other groups which are priority vulnerable groups in the children's centre area. (DCSF, 2007a: 12)

For example:

A children's centre provided outstanding support for families from the Traveller community on a local site. Once a week, and more frequently in the holidays, the centre's 'Smart Bus' visited with resources and activities for all age groups. (OfSTED, 2008b: 22).

As a result of this initiative the centre also prepared some of the mothers from the site for 'their theory driving test, using the laptop computers on the bus' (ibid.), the knock-on effect from this outreach work was that the community and the centre developed a relationship of mutual trust, the families made use of the mid-wives and health-care workers from the centre and, when the time came, both children and families felt more confident and positive about the children attending the local school. It is part of the mandate for Children's Centres that they ensure they have a clear understanding of what the needs of children and families in their local area are and that they plan for and target services to meet those needs. It is recognized that information to help this process can be gained through analysing statistical data 'such as population, deprivation, homelessness, demographic and ethnicity data' (DCSF, 2007a: 10), however, it is also recognized that a 'more real way' of knowing the needs of the community is through '"walking" the area, making contact with the families through key community groups, schools and normal points of contact like GP surgeries, health centres, and even libraries' (ibid.). Outreach work is essential in developing working relationships with families as it enables the community to understand what services are on offer and 'for those families who cannot or choose not to come into the centre, providing important information and access to services, thereby reducing the risk of exclusion' (DCSF, 2007a: 10).

Multi-agency working

As well as going out into the community to make links with children and families, ideally, on site a centre should have health visitors, midwives, family support workers, outreach workers, managers and volunteers (DCSF, 2007a: 16). Other on-site provision should be direct access to, or information about, local links to:

- early years provision;

- a childminder's network, including support for childminders;
- parenting education and family support services;
- education, training and employment services;
- health services; and access to wider services.
- drop-in sessions for parents and children, for example, 'stay and play' sessions, or Early Years provision; and
- links to Jobcentre Plus and health services (DCSF, 2007a: 15).

To further enhance the way multi-agency teams work together, all those working with families and their very young children should also be working to the Common Assessment Framework, this is 'a nationally standard approach to conducting an assessment of the needs of a child or young person and deciding how they should be met' (DCSF, 2007a: 17).

The Common Assessment Framework (CAF)

Ideally all agencies involved in working to support a child – including in terms of monitoring growth and development – should have access to the same files. In this way, under the CAF all agencies will be able to contribute their assessment information about the child and a holistic picture of the child's progress and needs can be kept. The CAF requires the various agencies to make assessments about the child in the three following 'domains':

- how well a child is developing, including in their health and progress in learning;
- how well parents or carers are able to support their child's development and respond appropriately to any needs;
- the impact of wider family and environmental elements on the child's development and on the capacity of their parents and carers, (CWDC, 2007: 20–21).

Consultation

It is a further requirement of Children's Centres that they should have an open consultative process that canvasses the views of all those that use them or might use them (DCSF, 2007a: 21). Not only should Children's Centres consult, but they must demonstrate how the results of their consultations are being responded to.

Working with parents – Early Years settings and schools

Having briefly outlined how Children's Centres have been working to develop relationships with families it is now up to the Early Year settings and schools who will be receiving children and parents from these centres, who are used to this sort of open and consultative dialogue about all aspects of their children's development, to continue to foster and develop the relationships that have been established.

Settings and schools are no strangers to working with parents and know that a good home/setting/school relationship in integral to the success of the setting or school and the enjoyment and achievement of the child (Bastiani and White, 2003: 4). Indeed, key findings from research (ibid.) shows that where there are good home/setting/school relationships:

- children achieve better long-term outcomes;
- that where settings and schools with a matched intake are compared, those with strong links with their parents achieve great success for their children; and
- in the same way, where settings and schools in similar areas are compared, where there are good links with parents there are fewer behaviour issues (Bastiani and White, 2003:4).

Activity

In strengthening relationships with parents many settings and schools set up a variety of meeting with parents. Below is a checklist of those elements that, if in place, can make for more mutually productive meetings. Read though the list and consider those which are usual practice in settings or schools you are familiar with.

- Meetings are arranged to suit the circumstances of parents, rather than the convenience of the setting or school, and only on weekdays.
- Some meetings are held outside the setting or school if this is helpful, for example in a in a community centre, church, mosque – this can be a very helpful strategy in developing relationships with different groups in the community.
- Parents *are encouraged to bring friends, family or members of community groups to meetings if this is helpful.*
- That where the meeting is about information about the setting or school, parents have the opportunity to respond to what is being said. It may be that this raises issues that cannot be dealt with there and then, so it is quite in order for the setting or school to respond by agreeing to take the point and pursue it outside this meeting.
- Meetings need to be positive events for all concerned. For example, where there may be reluctance between the setting or school and the parents, to talk about a child's progress, start by asking parents: '"Tell me one thing that you want me to know about your child's special talents." Parents will feel involved and valued' (Bastiani and White, 2003: 24).

In terms of wider initiatives, settings and schools can set up to foster links with parents. Many settings and schools:

- encourage parents to talk to adults in the setting or school when dropping off and collecting children;
- have developed home/setting/school schemes around literacy and numeracy support, for both children and parents, as necessary;
- will have a mixture of formal and informal reporting systems, where parents

are notified of children's success and, where they need support, this information will go to both parents, they are not living in the same home;

- send out information to parents and other contact with parents in a language other than English, where helpful;
- regularly invite parents into the setting or school for open days and to look at displays of work, and so on;
- run workshops on aspects of the curriculum and ideas on how parents can help support their children;
- run sessions on other multi-agency support available through the setting or school;
- hold workshops on ideas for managing children's behaviour and other advice parents may have asked for; and
- hold workshops on parents helping in the setting or classroom and on trips.

In terms of determining how settings and schools can enable children to enjoy and achieve in their learning we have focused on putting the child at the heart of the learning process through exploring personalized learning and AfL. We have also considered the need for settings and schools to have good relationships with parents to support this process. In many ways, we have focused on exploring achievement in terms of learning, but if a child is motivated, involved and interested in their learning, they will enjoy their learning. However, if we have any doubts that they are enjoying their learning, the simple solution it to ask the child about it, as the guidance for OfSTED inspectors states: 'in assessing children's levels of enjoyment, the range of evidence that inspectors consider includes children's enthusiasm, sense of fun, and expressions of pleasure and satisfaction from meeting challenges and doing well' (OfSTED, 2007a: 10).

Further reading 📖

Black, P. (2003) *Assessment for Learning: Putting it into Practice*. Maidenhead: McGraw-Hill Educational.

Black, P. and Williams, D. (2001) *Inside the Black Box*, http://ngfl.northumberland.gov.uk/keystage3ictstrategy/Assessment/blackbox.pdf

Children's Workforce Development Council (CWDC) (2007) *Common assessment framework for children and young people: practitioners' guide: Integrated working to improve outcomes for children and young people*. Leeds: Children's Workforce Development Council. Available at: www.everychildmatters.gov.uk/resources-and-practice/IG00063/

Useful websites 🖱

Advice on personalized learning: www.standards.dfes.gov.uk/personalisedlearning/

Advice on AfL: www.qca.org.uk/

Advice on working with parents and parents' entitlements under ECM: www.everychildmatters.gov.uk/

Making a Positive Contribution

This chapter explores:

- the importance of listening to children's voices and of involving them in decision-making processes;
- how to work with children to ensure they do not engage in acts of discrimination, or are subjected to such acts;
- how to help children develop self-confidence and deal with life-challenges, particularly transitions; and
- creating a sense of positive contribution to the wider community.

To meet the *Every Child Matters Outcomes Framework* (DCSF, 2008b) for making a positive contribution, Early Years settings and primary schools will need to be able to demonstrate that they are enabling children to: be engaged in decision-making and supporting the community and environment; develop positive relationships and choose not to bully or discriminate; enable children to develop self-confidence and successfully deal with life-changes and challenges.

Children's voice – engaging children in decision-making

Children spend a huge amount of their childhood in places of formal education, from Early Years settings, through primary school and into secondary school. Although these settings have children as their central and driving concern, children very often have little – if any – say or control in how these places are structured, organized and managed, or over what is provided in settings and school in terms of care and education (Wyness, 1999: 103). 'Adults take up education for children and are accountable to other adults for the educational services they provide … education policy clearly demonstrates that children are still the property of adults' (Wyness, 1999: 104). That we do not give children a voice – or one that is listened to and acted upon – in what is perhaps their lives most formative experience, says much about our actual model of what we believe a child to be. In the main, children's lives are structured and run by adults, usually children spend their time undertaking activities, at home as well as in Early Years settings and schools, that are organized and overseen by adults – even seemingly 'free play' activities. If children want to do something different, they must seek permission to do so, either from a parent, a carer, a practitioner, a teacher or another. Adults will also make decisions for children about where they go, what they do, who their friends should be and what they should wear. While many adults will maintain they do this as part of safeguarding children, the whole experience of parenting and childhood can sometimes seem to be resolving the tensions caused by adults trying to impose their rules and children trying to resist them.

In Chapter 5 we explored bullying through looking at what OfSTED (2008a) had researched children say about bullying. During an inspection OfSTED inspectors will routinely canvass the opinion of children on a range of issues to do with the setting or school. What the children say is used as evidence in preparing the final report. As part of the arrangements in the current inspection framework the inspecting team will write a letter for the children, explaining what the outcomes of the inspection are (OfSTED, 2008c). On surveying the impact of this strategy (OfSTED, 2006b), it was found that schools were passing the letters on to the children and the children had read them and thought the idea a good one. However, some of the younger children had problems understanding the content of the letter, because of the style in which it was written, and schools too acknowledged that they needed to develop their systems for better involving children in exploring what was raised in the letter (OfSTED, 2006b: 1). However, many schools were keen to follow-up with the children issues raised in the letters, but often needed to develop better systems for doing this (OfSTED, 2006b: 1). Where follow-up is successful, schools have used assembly time, class time – particularly citizenship lessons and circle time – as suitable vehicles for discussing the issues raised and any follow-up action being taken. Interestingly, OfSTED (2006b) found that head teachers were even more positive about the letters than the pupils, and where reservations about the scheme were expressed they came mainly from class teachers (OfSTED, 2006b: 3). In following-up the letters, the survey cites, as an example of good practice, a primary school that produced a 'child-friendly' version of the post-inspection action plan, with appropriately expressed success criteria which allowed children to 'trace their input during the inspection through to a key issue in the letter and a positive response by the school' (OfSTED, 2006b: 4).

In asking children about their lives and experiences it can seem from a child's point of view that they are constantly being told what to do – or even controlled – at every turn, by a 'battery of adults' (Thomas, 2000: 139), and they feel that it is only when they are away from adults they have the opportunity to make their own decisions and explore life in ways that are meaningful to them. In particular, children see formal education settings as places where they have very little power, often rules and decisions are made by adults, and particularly in schools, there is often little choice about what learning activities children are expected to engage with. Children can feel restricted in terms of the friendships they are allowed to have and the clothes they are allowed to wear, where they are allowed to go and what television programmes they are allowed to watch. Similarly, food can be another area of tension between adults and children, where again children feel the rules about what they can/cannot eat are set by adults. Often buying and preparing food is entirely part of the adult domain and there can be very little negotiation about what food is bought, prepared and served. Thomas in particular, also found that children feel adults do not listen to them: 'or not so attentively as they listen to other adults: they ignore them or leave them out of conversations; they interrupt, override, or redefine what they say' (Thomas, 2000: 143).

In many ways there are perfectly sound reasons for not letting children run their lives; these are very valid reasons to do with health and safety and adults not having access to limitless budgets. However, what adults often confuse here is the notion of what we might call licence and developing personal responsibility. It is often assumed that, without adults to guide and control children, children will not be able to distinguish between acting in excessive ways that may cause them harm and acting responsibly. It is also part of the dominant discourse with regard to the notion of 'children's voice' that promotes the assumption that if children are given a platform to influence decisions they will always go for eating the most unsuitable foods, watching the most unsuitable television programmes (and late into the night) wearing the most outrageous clothes and generally seeking to induce a state of anarchy.

Children are aware that adults believe they are too young to really understand the nature of some responsibilities, or are too young to be able to master some of the skills needed to run a household or their lives. Children understand about adult concerns about health and safety, but many feel adults can over-exaggerate the reality of these concerns and that adults are actually more interested in having their rules obeyed, rather than negotiating on issues. It may be the case that children have not yet acquired the level of vocabulary or articulation needed to verbally convince adults that they can take more responsibility than they are given – or at least have a valid opinion about how things should be done – or adults simply cannot, or do not want to, hear what children say. Although we know that, where there is no alternative, children take on very heavy loads of responsibility in some families, perhaps where there is a disabled parent, for example.

Children know their voices are not heard and are able to articulate and understand, probably better than adults, the consequences of not being listened too: 'when children are not listened to they may "get fed up", "give up and get depressed", or "develop a bad attitude"' (Thomas, 2000: 143). In terms of giving children a voice and letting them be part of controlling their own lives, there is also the need to help them learn to be independent and grow into self-reliant, resilient informed adults (Brannen, 2000: 154).

Why do children need a voice?

For some adults there are very real power issues and concerns about giving up what they see as their authority to children and, worse, believing that their authority is being undermined by a child. In talking to children about this issue, research shows that children have a good insight into where the power lies in decision-making, that while they are aware that they 'have rights' many feel overwhelmed by adult power. Children understand too, that:

> 'it is our life – we have our own feelings, concerns and views, and the outcomes will affect us'; 'it is fairer' 'you feel more included and it prevents you getting angry or sad that adults aren't listening'; 'it leads to better decisions' 'adults are able to listen to you and find out what you want, and more likely to make a decision that you are happy with'; 'you gain information' 'you can find out what is going on'; 'you learn from it' 'you gain experience, skills and confidence, learn how to speak up and take more responsibility, learn from your mistakes, and become more confident'; 'it leads to positive changes' 'things can get sorted out and problems 'nipped in the bud'. (Thomas, 2000: 151)

In terms of children being safe, there are concerns, too, that if children do not feel they have a voice, or will not be listened to, they will not seek help when they need it. In giving children a voice, the challenge for adults in this situation, is how best to work with children of different ages and at different stages of development, to enable them to participate in decision-making processes in ways that are mutually beneficial. Where settings and schools have explored the idea of children's voice and have given children more say in decision-making processes, what has been found is that: 'children turn out to be capable of much more than adults think' (Foley et al., 2001: 84). 'Children as young as two years of age have been able to tell researchers from the Day Care Trust that the things they liked about their day care included good food, their friendships with other children and being able to make their own choices' (ibid.).

Children are also very adept at knowing which adults are more likely to listen to them and give them a voice and which are more reluctant to do so, again, perhaps rather worryingly, 'teachers were often singled out as particularly bad at listening to children' (Thomas, 2000: 143).

School Councils

One of the most successful and popular ways of involving children in the day-to-day running of schools, for many schools, is to set up a school council. For information on how to set up a council there are a number of websites (see below) that offer advice, guidance and support. School councils can also become part of a national network of School Councils which will provide support for new councils and information about successful initiatives. School Councils provide an excellent opportunity for children to develop a platform that gives them a voice in the school. However a successful School Council will take time to develop. If the children have no experience of being involved in such initiatives it will need time to work with them to help them understand how councillors might be chosen/elected, how council meetings could be run, including the need for agendas and notes of meetings, and how councillors are going to consult with their constituents to represent them on issues and feed back information to them. Thought also needs to be given to how the council will ensure all children, from all age groups have a voice and that younger children are not marginalized by the older children. The school needs also to be prepared to give real power to the council. For the council to be successful the children need to see that its decisions are impacting on school life. The organization School Councils UK publishes some very good activity guides for children to help get them started.

Initially children will also need help in setting up protocols for:

- knowing which groups in the school it would be helpful to liaise with and keep informed about council activity, for example: the Senior Management Team, the Governing Body, the Parent Teacher Association, class teachers and lunchtime supervisors;
- deciding how this liaison is to happen needs some thought too – will there be some communication after each meeting, will representatives from these groups be allowed to meetings, or invited depending on what is being discussed?

As with all initiatives how the council is to be initially set up and run requires planning – and children need to be involved at this point. It is likely that at least one adult will be heavily involved initially in supporting and setting up the council, but ideally, over time, as the children grasp the idea of what powers they have and how they can be exercised democratically, the children can increasingly be left to their own devices, consulting with adults in the ways suggested above.

Where School Councils are particularly successful is where schools have used the Citizenship curriculum to discuss issues of democracy and negotiation. Children have experience through this aspect of the curriculum to explore putting forward ideas, presenting a case, ways of voting and the need to sometimes renegotiate initial ideas in the face of opposition, or work towards compromises that better benefit a larger number of people than the initial idea.

Case study

In 2006 a primary school in West Sussex set up a their School Council giving it, as its first task, the issue of how to 'spend' the games and sports equipment vouchers collected from a large supermarket chain. Staff briefed the older children about the possible ways the council could be constructed and councillors selected or elected from the different classes in the school. These children then discussed the notion of a council and councillors with the younger children. To ensure the youngest children were represented, older children nominated themselves to be a 'Buddy Councillor'. For the purposes of the council meetings and consultation the Buddy Councillors would work with the younger children representing their views as necessary. Overtime, as the younger children became more confident and understood the process, they became less reliant on their buddies. The children, through the council decided the vouchers would be used to buy in equipment for each class to use at breaktimes, each class choosing its own equipment.

As with any new venture there were teething problems and much negotiation and re-negotiation, but this was an important learning process in itself. Now the council is more mature it has taken on other initiatives, many of which have come from suggestions from the children; for example: giving over an area of the school grounds to grow vegetables, re-organizing how children come into assembly and where they sit and what assembly themes might be.

The council has also become a good source for the school for canvassing the children's voice or when children are needed to represent the school. For example, during the recent OfSTED inspection, councillors were able to take inspectors around the school and talk about initiatives they had been involved in; they could explain how the council 'worked' and show them agendas and minutes of their meetings.

Mature School Councils are also a very good way of getting children involved in the wider community, in its Activity Guide 02, *Getting Involved in the Wider Community*, the School Councils UK organization suggests councils try some of the ideas listed below.

1. Research ideas and initiatives for meeting and working with: local residents, local businesses, care homes, community groups, the police, possibly even local government or the parish council and the constituency's Member of Parliament.
2. In some instances there are already community issues that are being pursued by local groups, many of whom would welcome the support of the local school's council, for example over such issues as threatened closure of local hospitals/post offices, public transport concerns, issues with local leisure facilities and the environment (School Councils UK, 2008b).

Develop self-confidence, resilience and dealing with life-changes

One of the consequences of not involving children more directly in what is happening in their lives is that we risk alienating them, the long-term results of which can, in the most extreme cases, lead to truancy, exclusion 'problems of child protection and child crime ... youthful violence and children on the street' (Wyness, 1999: 100). On the other hand, working with children, listening to their voice, responding to their concerns and giving them power in decision-making processes has immediate and long-term benefits in terms of developing confidence and resilience – 'the ability to rebound from crisis and overcome life challenges' (Walsh, 2006: ix). When children are given the opportunity to be proactive in determining what is happening around them, the skills they learn from the experience have a knock-on effect in all aspects of their lives. Very few children and families go through a life that is without challenges; most human beings, across the course of their lives, experience one or more adverse events (Walsh, 2006: ix). It is an unusual family that does not experience some event that challenges its sense of well-being and might be an event that, at the time, seems too overwhelming to deal with. Besides the unexpected and unwanted events that happen to all of us, many children will be born into families that seem to already have things stacked against them – poverty, issues of child protection and the challenges that come from being a refugee, an asylum seeker family, living in isolated ethnic minorities, having a disability or having to care for a disabled parent.

Where children have already had the experience of 'having a voice' and have built up self-confidence and resilience, they are better prepared to deal with challenging events. Further to this, where families too are used to being listened to and supported, they too develop resilience which can help them come through adverse situations and go on to survive and succeed.

Walsh in exploring the concept of resilience states: 'I grew up in a family challenged by many adversities. It took a long time to appreciate my parents' struggles and their remarkable courage, perseverance, and resourcefulness' (Walsh, 2006: x). In his work Walsh (2006) explores how the dominant discourse of what constitutes a 'perfect' family has led to overlooking the very positive personal resources families have to see them through challenging times; that it has been the 'mission' of those seeking to help to 'fix' the family and assume that the problems will then disappear. We have already explored some aspects of the notion of resilience and the idea that there are no such things as ideal families and, similarly, there are no simple solutions to the challenges that some families face. Where families are helped to deal with their challenges is where those supporting them listen to their voice and work with what the family need to help them through their problems – 'what matters most are effective family processes' (Walsh, 2006: xi): 'all families have the potential for adaptation, repair, and growth. A family resilience approach provides a positive and pragmatic framework that guides interventions to strengthen family processes for resilience as presenting problems are addressed' (Walsh, 2006: xiv).

Giving children too much information

One of the concerns over giving children a voice is that childhood should be a time of innocence and freedom from responsibility. However, as explored in Chapter 2, it is only to adults that children are 'innocent' and only because adults 'know' what it is children do not 'know'. The 'loss' of innocence occurs, only in the eyes of adults when children acquire certain forms of knowledge and experience. What this particular body of knowledge or form of experience might be, that leads to loss of innocence, is relative to culture and history. In this way, children are not 'innocent' but simply ignorant of things adults prefer to keep them ignorant of, and there is the concern that ignorance can, of itself, cause harm. Two areas of knowledge and understanding that often fall into this category are those often termed 'sex and drugs'. However, as we have seen in Chapter 5, part of enabling children to remain safe from some forms of abuse, in this instance through sex and drugs, is that they must know something of these things, to protect themselves. As we explored in Chapter 4, the idea that children, particularly children as young as 3 begin to learn about relationship and sex can cause concern amongst some adults. Discussions about what children should and should not be told about relationships and sex focuses many of the feelings that adults have about the notion of children's voice generally. We know that children are vulnerable and yet we want them to grow-up and be independent, responsible, informed adults, this further exacerbates the tension between what they should be told and when. The situation is further complicated by the overwhelming access to sexual images and examples of sexual encounters that children have through the media.

In reality, it is more or less impossible to censor information; indeed, in many instances it is not necessary. Where children are consulted and their voices have an impact on what is happening in their lives it is possible to work with children to help them deal with the information they are encountering, whatever its source, in an informed way. Where a child is denied a voice and lives in a world that is demarcated and controlled entirely by adults, be that in education settings or at home, the child will grow up less able to make informed choices between appropriate and inappropriate, harmless and harmful, behaviours and actions.

Transition

An example of one of the positive benefits of helping children to develop a sense of self and resilience, through enabling them to have a voice, is in how this empowers children to deal with life-changes, such as transitions. Moving from one familiar set of circumstances to another can be challenging for children and adults alike. While for many children 'starting nursery/playgroup' or 'starting school' can be very exciting, even the most resilient child benefits from some help to manage these transition points – as do their parents. In their educational career, children and families have a number of transition points to manage, while for a school or setting they may be focused on only one or two points, at most. For the child initially there is moving from home to nursery or playgroup; then from nursery to school. For some children, where the infant and junior school are two separate schools there may be a further transition at this point – and then there is the move to secondary school. All transitions have a lead into period and then an adjustment time once the transition has happened. Research increasingly shows that where children and families are well prepared to know what to expect and then well supported once the transition is complete, the children cope better, both in terms of well-being and learning progression.

For any setting or school considering its transition arrangements, the two main factors to be aware of are briefly outlined below:

- **Pastoral support** for the child and family – this will involve visiting the new school or setting, knowing where things are and who people are, where the toilets are, where the rooms are, what playground to use, where to have lunch, can parents come in with the children and hang up their coats? Where are pushchairs to be parked? What to wear, what to wear for PE, are crisps allowed in lunch boxes? The list can seem endless, but reflects the very real concerns about going somewhere new, that children and parents have.
- **Changes in the curriculum and teaching styles** – as children move through the transition points between the changing phases in their learning, they have to adjust to different ways in which learning activities are presented to them. The curriculum at the various stages differs and traditionally the various phases of education have adopted different teaching styles in curriculum delivery. These changes, if they are not well managed, can cause considerable disruption in a child's learning journey and adversely affect their self-confidence.

In 2007 OfSTED published a report on the transition arrangements of 144 Foundation Stage settings it had surveyed. From its survey it identified the following benchmarks for good practice.

Where transition into, and out of, the setting is *well done*, it is where the following aspects of good practice are in place:

- Home visits are made and any particular need a child or family has is noted and supportive arrangements are made, including being aware of the needs of working parents.
- A range of activities are planned including joint activities between the setting and schools – staff from the school visit the setting 'including catering staff

and the school crossing patrol' (OfSTED, 2007b: 22). 'Children attending the pre-school visited the receiving school regularly and the Reception class visited the pre-school setting for events such as picnics. Parents and practitioners shared the children's records of achievements which were passed to the school to inform practitioners about each child' (OfSTED, 2007b: 22).

- A 'buddy' system was in place to support children through transition.
- Almost half of the settings said that children with identified needs received good support from outside agencies across the points of transfer: 'Home visits, meetings with parents, links with the Sure Start team, health visitors, the asylum seeker team and other agencies ensured children and their parents had a calm introduction into life in the nursery' (OfSTED, 2007b: 25).

Transition into and out of the setting had been *less effective* where the following issues outlined below have not been addressed:

- Promoting progress in learning at points of transition was less effective.
- Parents – particularly working parents who find 'staggered' transition arrangements difficult to fit around their work.
- Some settings had sought to prepare children for the transfer to school by providing what they considered to be the sorts of learning activities the children would encounter at school, including 'providing more direct teaching and expecting children to sit for longer' (OfSTED, 2007b: 22). This practice is counselled against, since it is inappropriate for the age of the children, the teaching seen was not engaging and increasingly many schools, particularly in their Foundation Stage adopt a teaching approach more in line with the systems used in Early Years settings.
- Settings that do not have a policy on transition, and simply build on their previous practice. With a properly considered policy, children, parents and staff can be consulted on what works well and what can be developed, plus elements such as those above can be written in to ensure nothing is omitted.
- It would seem that there is still very little training in this area of provision. Some local authorities have recognized the need for providing advice and information about transition. However, as with many things, provision is enhanced by appropriate training (OfSTED, 2007b: 22).

Success in managing transition points in school

Many of the pastoral elements discussed above are also successfully used by schools to manage that aspect of transition for children and families. Schools make home visits, and provide the opportunity for children and parents to come into the school to spend time there getting to know staff, routines and where things are. Many schools, are increasingly recognizing the benefit of initially adopting the teaching approaches of the phase that the children are coming from and then, once the children are settled into the other aspects of school life, moving the children over to the teaching practices that better suit the phase they are now in. Most schools that have a Reception class or a

Foundation Stage organized along the lines of an Early Years setting, where learning activities are play and experience based and children are linked to a key worker. Some schools will continue to use this approach for the first term in Key Stage 1 and then gradually move towards more traditional infant school teaching approaches that better suit the nature of the National Curriculum. Where this form of continuity works best is where Foundation Stage staff also have the opportunity to work alongside Year 1 colleagues (OfSTED, 2007b: 22). Such practices have been mirrored by some secondary schools, who have recon-figured teaching in Year 7 and sometimes into Year 8, to be more in line with teaching approaches more associated with primary schools.

Other examples of good practice that are being used are:

- where colleagues across transition points can meet to discuss planning to ensure there is progression in learning; and
- procedures children have become used to are continued, registration processes, for example. As an example of good practice OfSTED (2007b: 23) cite:

> Arriving in Foundation Stage 1, children registered themselves by finding their photograph and putting it onto a number ladder. This was used as a focus for checking how many children were present during the more formal registration session. In Foundation Stage 2, self-registration was extended. Using an interactive whiteboard, the children moved photographs of them-selves to indicate whether they wanted a school dinner or a packed lunch. These sets were later counted separately and developed the children's count-ing skills to 20 and beyond.

Case study

In 2007 in a school in West Sussex one of the teaching assistants was given the responsibility of co-ordinating elements of the children's transfer from local playgroups, nurseries and other settings into the Reception class in the school. As part of her work she worked with the Reception children to make a book for the children that would be transferring to the school that September. She asked the children to think about what it was like for them coming to school and what the 'new' children would find it most helpful to know.

The book was to be a series of photographs with captions. The teaching assistant and the children identified a list of things that could go in the book, including photographs and names of teachers, teaching assistants, lunchtime supervisors and the head teacher. There were also pictures of the children doing different activities, playing, reading in the reading corner, playing with the 'big' children in the playground, having lunch, and so on.

The book was produced in an A4 format – although, ideally, the teaching assistant wanted it in a 'big book' format. Each page was in colour and laminated

continued

continued

to make it durable. Enough copies were made so that each of the settings the children would be coming from could have a copy. The teaching assistant took the book to the settings with Reception children, where possible, and talked through the book with the nursery children and answered their questions. The books were in the settings and were purpose designed so the young children could look through them as part of their day-to-day activities and talk to friends and key workers about the pictures. Once they had been on their visits to the school, they could then use the books as a reference to talk about what they had seen, what school was 'really' like and ask about things that they were still unsure of.

Learning progression and practitioner and teacher expectations

Research and anecdotal evidence suggests that colleagues in the different phases of the educational process are notoriously bad at using the records about children that they are given at transition points. Many settings and schools, including secondary schools, will say this is because they like to 'start from scratch' (OfSTED, 2007b: 24). Sometimes this happens because the school or setting is receiving children from a number of different places and the records they receive are all different, or have not been kept in the way the school would want or expect. It takes time to understand how information is being presented and making sense of what useful things it might contain about a child's learning and development. The problems are further compounded where the transition also necessitates a change in curriculum documentation. So, for example, practitioners in Early Years settings will worry about how playgroups and childminders have kept records. And Key Stage 1 teachers are sometimes not aware of the usefulness of the information in the Foundation Stage profile (FSP) as it records progress in terms of Language, Literacy and Communication whereas in Key Stage 1 progress is monitored and assessed in terms of Speaking and Listening, Reading and Writing (OfSTED, 2004: 2). In real terms, these are not insurmountable objects, the curriculum from the EYFS framework does lead in to the National Curriculum, but for practitioners, teachers and others already feeling hard pressed to meet all aspects of learning and safeguarding provision, taking useful information from previous records can seem a requirement too far. The Office for Standards in Education (2007b) do report that Key Stage 1 (KS1) teachers are getting better at using information in the FSP, particularly to plan work for the autumn term. The Office for Standards in Education (2004: 2) further comments that this aspect of transition could be better accomplished by greater involvement of subject coordinators, particularly in terms of working with Foundation Stage and KS1 colleagues to look at long-term planning in subject areas.

There is generally good practice in making use of records that document and monitor progress where:

- colleagues on either side of the transition point had the opportunity to discuss the information;
- settings and schools actually received the information; and
- parents too were involved in the process.

Buddying and peer mentoring

Examples of engaging children in initiatives that enable them to be proactive members of the school and wider community include children providing support for one another, through such schemes as: 'buddying' or befriending services between pupils to encourage positive relationships and friendships; or counselling support, where, in some instances, specific conflicts between pupils in school are dealt with by pupils trained in conflict resolution.

Activity

Many settings and schools use buddying or peer-mentoring schemes. Below is a checklist of what works well in these schemes. Use the list to audit the schemes you may be familiar with – or to consider those aspects of the list you would want to adopt as part of your practice.

- Children are trained and designated as 'on duty' during break times and can normally be found within certain designated areas of the playground.
- In some instances Buddies will have been 'trained to intercede where there are low-level disputes such as name calling, general verbal disagreements and threatening behaviour between pupils' – and their training will include trying to mediate or knowing when to seek assistance from adults to resolve the issue.
- Buddies will instigate 'playground games' and actively encourage 'lone' children and others to join in (OFSTED, 2008a; Wyness, 1999: 107).

A further important feature of allowing children to take on such roles is that it acknowledges that children have the competence and skills to undertake the role. It does not presuppose that these roles can only be fulfilled by adults.

Contributing to the wider community and community cohesion

In 2007 the DCSF published the document *Guidance on the Duty to Promote Community Cohesion*. The document provides settings and schools with guidance about what community cohesion means, why it is important and examples of what community cohesion might be.

The notion of community cohesion is rooted in the aims and principles of the curriculum documents that settings and schools are already using to support aspects of their provision for children and their families, particularly the aspects of the curriculum that deal with personal, social and emotional education and citizenship. The notion of community cohesion is also directly linked to the fourth aspect of the Every Child Matters outcomes for well-being, that of enabling children to make a positive contribution to the wider community, both as children and in the future as adults.

The DSCF define cohesion, in this instance as being: 'about how to avoid the corrosive effects of intolerance and harassment: how to build a mutual civility among different groups, and to ensure respect for diversity alongside a commitment to common and shared bonds' (DCSF, 2007b: 4). Through this aspect of the ECM agenda, the DCSF is looking to settings and schools to work with children and their families to enable them to live and work in 'a country which is diverse in terms of cultures, religions or beliefs, ethnicities and social backgrounds (DCSF, 2007b: 3). It is envisaged that, although Britain is a diverse society it is possible to create a *sense of belonging* and a *common vision* that overrides difference. In this way, all children and families will then be able to access the advantages and benefits which are potentially available to all. Settings and schools are uniquely placed to help develop the sense of community cohesion since they are already acting as a 'hub' of community activity. Settings and schools draw children and families from their immediate local communities; they provide extended services that may draw a wider range of people to the setting or school, other than the local children and families. For example, other community groups will use the buildings and other services that are available through the setting or school, be they for health, leisure or learning activities.

There are three particular aspects of setting and school provision through which this object can be achieved. First, through the learning activities children are engaged in, particularly those that are part of personal, social and emotional education and citizenship. Here, there is already provision for children to learn about understanding others and diversity as well as exploring issues that promote shared vales, such as human rights and the responsibilities that go hand-in-hand with holding rights.

The second way in which settings and schools can promote community cohesion is through what the DCSF have called 'Equity and excellence' and this links directly to many of the areas already covered in this book. That is to say, since September 2007, through *Guidance on the Duty to Promote Community Cohesion* it has been the duty of settings and schools: 'to ensure equal opportunities for all to succeed at the highest level possible, striving to remove barriers to access and participation in learning and wider activities and working to eliminate variations in outcomes for different groups' (DCSF, 2007b: 7).

Thirdly, community cohesion is to be promoted through engagement with and development of the extended services already offered by settings and schools. Such services can be vehicles for providing children and their families with opportunities to meet, through taking part in a variety of activities, bringing together a diverse range of people in their communities. In this way, diversity is meant not only in terms of culture and ethnicity, but also in terms of age and class. For example, a school may host a community group engaging in an environmental project in the local area. Groups such as these bring together a wide range of diverse community members and provide a common purpose and shared values which transcend all diversity.

Activity

Guidance on the Duty to Promote Community Cohesion the DCSF (2007b) outline a range of activities settings and schools can be engaged in particularly in terms of promoting **equity and excellence**.

Read through the ideas below and use it as a checklist to consider those activities you have seen being promoted in a setting or school.

People from the wider community, for example police community support officers, local councillors, community leaders, librarians from the local library, the local children's centre community outreach worker, representatives from local businesses, local environmental groups, and so on, regularly come in to the setting or school to directly support learning, lead assemblies or provide 'updates' on what has been happening since their last visit.

There are structured and formalized links with established local businesses or community groups which enable a symbiotic relationship between them and the community to develop. For example, as part of its extended services the setting or school runs an environmental club, for children and their families. The club is run by those linked to the environmental group in the community, and children and parents are invited to engage in activities in the wider community. Similarly, the adult education service runs sessions to support parents for whom English is an additional language and asks the same parents for their help in using their ability to speak languages other than English to work with others in the community.

Children go out into the community to help in voluntary community-based activities.

Engagement with parents through curriculum evenings, teaching and learning activities such as parent and child courses, and family liaison work, tailored to suit the needs and requirements of the school and parents. For example, reaching parents who may need additional support through other local bodies and community points of contact. (DCSF, 2007b: 10)

Further reading

Alderson, P. (2000) *Young Children's Rights: Exploring Beliefs, Principles and Practice*. London: Jessica Kingsley.

Department for Children, Schools and Families (DCSF) (2007b) *Guidance on the Duty to Promote Community Cohesion*. London: DCSF.

Department for Children, Schools and Families (DCSF) (2008c) *Working Together:*

Listening to the Voices of Children and Young People. London: DCSF.

Klein, R. (2003) *We Want Our Say.* Stoke-on-Trent: Trentham.

Useful websites

www.schoolcouncils.org/

www.schoolcouncilswales.org.uk/

8

Achieving Economic Well-being

This chapter explores:

- factors that mitigate against economic well-being including poverty, race and class;
- how, with appropriate family support, children can be enabled to achieve economic well-being; and
- how extended services can better help children and families achieve economic well-being.

The *Every Child Matters Outcomes Framework* (DCSF, 2008b) for enabling children and families to achieve economic well-being requires that Early Years settings and primary schools must demonstrate that they are supporting children and families in ways that encourage children to achieve in their learning and begin to understand the lifelong benefits of learning. They must also be able to demonstrate that they are supporting children and their families in living in decent homes in sustainable communities and that children and families that are living in poverty, or do not have access to transport and material goods, are being supported in working to change these circumstances.

In most ways, enabling children themselves to achieve economic well-being is a long-term goal – particularly from the standpoint of Early Years settings and primary schools. However, we have already looked at a range of factors, that if not 'got right' for children in their earliest years, will go on to have a long-term effect on their chances at achieving the five ECM outcomes. We have also explored how children who grow up in healthy, safe environments and know how to manage their own health and safety, will be better enabled to thrive and achieve in educational terms. Similarly, we have looked at how enabling children to enjoy and achieve in learning and education – again, beginning in the earliest years – will also encourage children to pursue learning as a way of achieving long-term well-being, eventually being better placed to achieve economic well-being for themselves. While we work with children and families to help them attain the ECM outcomes in the long term, for young children their immediate experience of economic well-being is very much linked to that of their families and, therefore, much of the support children need to achieve economic well-being in the present will be influenced by how settings and schools support families in increasing their access to training, education, employment, decent homes, sustainable communities and in being able to increase their incomes.

Poverty

At the beginning of this book we explored how, as a just society, we are concerned that all are enabled to have access to the goods that such a society can offer, be that health, education and material goods. However, we also explored that, despite numerous policies since the inception of the welfare state, there are still children and families living in poverty, which not only affects the short-term well-being of children and families, but also has negative long-term health, educational and economic effects on well-being (Grusky, 2005: 1).

Poverty can be measured through the Human Development Index (HDI) which takes as a starting point an individual's income and can, by the use of a weighted formula, including factoring in an individual's age, education and postcode give an indicator of the degree of that individuals affluence or otherwise and also make predictions about life-expectancy (Grusky, 2005: 11). Another way of measuring poverty, particularly in determining whether an individual or family is experiencing poverty in economic terms, is in measuring the family's income against the cost, at any one time, of a notional basic 'food basket' (Rakodi, 2002: 4), although there is some debate as to the usefulness of this way of determining level of poverty. The idea of the 'basic food basket' assesses a family's poverty level calculated in terms of their ability to buy food and other essential goods, regarded as those needed to attain a minimum or average level of well-being in the population within which they live where 'minimum consumption requirements are typically based on the food expenditure necessary to attain some recommended food energy intake' (Rakodi, 2002: 5). Poverty is also sometimes defined as: having an income which is less than 60 per cent of the national average (excluding the wealthiest members of society) (Knight, 2005). The 2006–07 figures published by the Department for Work and Pensions (2008) show that the mean income for households in Britain, before housing costs was approximately £24,000 per year (approximately £463 per week) and that the median income, before housing costs, was £19,600 per year (approximately £377 per week). The same report shows that 12.8 per cent of children are living in poverty (DWP, 2008: 61). The Communities and Local Government (2008) Indices of Deprivation, ranks district council areas throughout England in terms of levels of deprivation, the latest figures, published for 2007, show that of the 354 district councils in England, in 2007 the top three most deprived areas were Liverpool, Hackney and Tower Hamlets, with Manchester coming fourth. In the middle of the table are North East Derbyshire (176th), Mid Devon (177th) and Trafford (178th), with the most affluent local authority households being South Northamptonshire (351st), Surrey Heath (352nd), Wokingham (353rd) and Hart (Hampshire) (354th).

Activity

To find out more about the levels of poverty and deprivation in your area you can access the Deprivation Index at: www.communities.gov.uk/communities/

Further information about poverty and deprivation is available to schools through information sent to each school every year by OfSTED. Each year OfSTED compile information for each school that provides analysis of the school's and pupils' performance data. This report is known as RAISE – Reporting and Analysis for Improvement through School Self-evaluation. (It has replaced OfSTED's Performance and Assessment (PANDA) reports and the DCSF's Pupil Achievement Tracker (PAT)).

The report provides information about the economic health of the area which the children come from and breaks down the pupil's end of key stage tasks and teacher assessment tests results by subject, gender and ethnicity. It shows how well the children are achieving against national averages and against schools in similar economic circumstances.

Some head teachers share the information in the report with their staff, since it helps with target-setting and school improvement. General information and examples of anonymous RAISE packages can be found on the OfSTED website at: www.raiseonline.org/login.aspx?ReturnUrl=%2findex.aspx

It is worth bearing in mind that any statistics will tell only part of the story and some statistics will mask factors – for example, even in seemingly very affluent areas there will be pockets of deprivation, and vice versa. Similarly some surveys do not identify groups that are particularly at risk of poverty, for example, households where there are disabled adults or children. Also measuring poverty only in terms of economic factors does not take into account other assets families possess, like houses, the skills of the individuals in the household and the social networks the household can draw on. Having a range of such assets can mitigate what might seem to be monetary poverty (Rakodi, 2002).

Poverty is so debilitating for households because not only does it impact on immediate and long-term well-being, but it also reduces a family's resilience in terms of being able to withstand unexpected crisis, stresses and shocks.

Until recently most parts of the developing world have enjoyed increased financial security and rises in disposable income, since the end of the Second World War. However, while national trends have shown increases in incomes overall, this again can mask what has been happening for individual families. Walsh (2006) claims: the financial prospects of most young families today are lower than those of their parents, 'with a decline in median income and more families living in poverty' (Walsh, 2006: 35). Similarly the national picture does not take into account the fact that, for most households, currently at least two incomes are needed to support the family. Further factors to consider are, for example, in Britain over the past 30 years there have been considerable changes in the employment opportunities available. This has been due to rapid changes in technology making some jobs redundant and the decline of industries such as coal-mining and shipbuilding. In 1947 the coal-mining industry employed 750,000 people (BBC, 1999), but through the mid-1980s and early 1990s pits were closed as coal-mining was becoming economically unviable. The final blow came to the industry in 1993 when 30 pits were closed with the loss of 30,000 jobs and the remaining part of the industry privatized. While the government did pledge money to help those affected by job losses, because whole families and communities relied on the pits for their livelihood, still there was considerable economic devastation in some areas (BBC, 1999). In this way, while communities can support small numbers of families in poverty, the problems become harder when it is whole communities that suddenly face adverse changes in their economic circumstances. Change occurs in national patterns of work available, as the importance of industries rises and falls; for example, over the past 30 years there has been general change in British industry from steel, coal and manufacturing to service industries. Such changes can mean significant changes in economic conditions and job prospects, which can have a destructive impact on family stability and well-being (McLanahan, Garfinkel and Mincy, in Haskins 2001).

There have been other demographic changes that have had their impact on poverty issues too. While it is without a doubt a great benefit that health has improved and generally people are living longer, where individuals have not planned for their retirement many may be anticipating an impoverished old age. For some families this will lead to households containing people across three, four or even five generations as older family members become reliant on others for financial support. When only some of these generations can work, this adds to the financial strain. Ageing also brings with it increased likelihood of chronic illnesses and disability. These either pose stressful family caregiving challenges as families seek to support their elderly relatives, or leave those without families vulnerable to living on low incomes (Walsh, 2006: 36).

The livelihoods of the poor are determined predominantly by the geographical context in which they live and the constraints and opportunities this location presents. This is because context – economic, environmental, social and political – largely determines the assets accessible to people, how they can use these and, thus, their ability to obtain secure livelihoods.

Race and ethnicity

As we have explored the demography of Britain has changed considerably since 1945, no more so than in terms of the increased diversity of races and ethnicities that now form the British population. The 2001 Census has shown that nearly one in eight pupils comes from a minority ethnic background. By 2010, the proportion is expected to be around one in five (DfES, 2003a: 8). As the changes in the cultural dynamics of Britain began to impact on dominant discourses in the 1950s, much research has been undertaken to explore the experience of ethnic minority groups in Britain. While there is evidence that Britain is a thriving multi-ethnic island, there is also overwhelming evidence that there are tensions between ethnic groups and there is still a strong link between ethnicity, the chances of living in poverty and underachievement at school: 'which will determine ... success in later life. These factors will affect whether or not [children] go to university, get a good job and the contribution they make to society' (DfES, 2003a: 8; Henry, 2004; Walsh, 2006).

It was the Mcpherson report (Knowles, 2006), Lord Mcpherson's summing up of the inquiry into the racist murder of the London teenager Stephen Lawrence in 1993, that first highlighted the impact on lives of institutionalized racism in Britain. Mcpherson states that many organizations fail to provide appropriate professional services to people, because of their colour, culture and ethnic origin; that because of deeply held and unacknowledged, values, beliefs and attitudes held by those in the organization, some behave in a way that discriminates against others and disadvantages minority ethnic people (Henry, 2004: 2; Knowles, 2006: 24). In this way two of the most defining features of the ethnic minority experience in Britain has been limited employment opportunities, which has often meant working in low-wage menial jobs (Henry, 2004: 11), the knock-on effects of this being that this leads to poor housing and poverty.

In 2003 in its publication, *Aim Higher: Raising the Attainment of Ethnic Minority Pupils*, the DfES found that Chinese and Indian children were achieving better than the national average, however, children from black Caribbean and Pakistani backgrounds were doing significantly worse. In contrast, half of 'White, Indian and Chinese pupils went on to achieve at least five good GCSE passes, the same is true for just three in ten Black Caribbean children and four in ten of those of Pakistani or Black African origin' (DfES, 2003a). The report also acknowledged the link between the impact of poverty and children failing to thrive in terms of their education and recognized the need for proactive policies to raise the attainment of ethnic minority children. There is also considerable research that shows certain ethnic minority groups are considerably underachieving in educational terms. Legislation to help tackling this underachievement was further strengthened by the passing of the 2000 Race Relations (Amendment) Act (RRAA), which required all organizations to proactively tackle the issue of racism (Knowles, 2006: 25). As a result of this legislation all settings and schools have been required to have polices that outline their approach to dealing with incidents of racism, where they occur and how the setting or school will proactively seek to promote equality of opportunity for all and promote good race relations. In terms of working directly to raise underachievement in ethnic minority pupils, the DfES stated that to be effective in this area of their provision settings and school needed:

- direction from a strong manager or head teacher and leadership team who proactively established a whole-setting/school strategy on the issue;
- that all those involved in working with the children should have high expectations for achievement, for example, where a child may have English as an additional language (EAL) there must be strategies in place to support that child – not to marginalize them 'until they can speak English';
- to ensure that learning activities are planned to be effective for all children, having cultural relevance to the children and bilingual support, where necessary;
- close and direct links with families and the wider local community who, in turn, are encouraged to play a full part in the life of the setting or school (DfES, 2003a: 5).

Since 2003 OfSTED have undertaken follow-up research (2005d) *Race Equality in Education: Good Practice in Schools and Local Education Authorities* (OfSTED, 2005d) to explore good practice in providing for underachieving groups of children. The report outlines the good practice seen in schools, and expects these principles to be applied across all educational settings. OfSTED identify good practice in supporting children from different ethnic minorities as happening where:

- the school has an inclusive approach towards meeting the needs of all children as individuals and does not see ethnicity as a 'bolt-on' extra need;
- attainment data – such as that available through RAISE is used effectively to look at trends in terms of achievement of children from different ethnic backgrounds and appropriate strategies are put in place to improve children's experiences;
- race equality issues are tackled overtly through the curriculum, in such subjects as Personal and Social Education and Citizenship, and through the exploration of a wider range of topics in the arts and humanities;
- staff have undertaken training to enable them to better deal with race-related incidents, helping them to develop knowledge, confidence, skills and understanding of different types of incidents, making it easier for staff to handle, record and resolve conflicts' (OfSTED, 2005d: 3);
- the most effective schools are those that make strong links with ethnic minority groups in the local community; these have the knock-on effect of not only supporting attainment, but also pupils' well-being (OfSTED, 2005d: 3).

Activity

All settings and schools are required to have a policy for dealing with racism. Some settings and schools will feel that since they are mainly white, the issues of racism are less relevant to them. However, it is often where racism is not addressed or mentioned that it can be at its worst, simply thinking 'it doesn't happen here' is a form of institutional racism in itself.

Read through your setting's, or school's policy. When was it last updated? Does it cover the most recent legislation that it needs to?

Not only does racism occur in overt ways – that is, though obvious racist behaviour – but also by marginalizing and ignoring diversity in all areas of the setting and school life.

In your work in a setting or school is it routine that inclusion of race equality concepts in learning activities is part of day-to-day practice? Does the learning environment reflect the diversity of the area or of Britain? When specific activities are planned, do they have a wide cultural basis from which they are drawn, or are cultures other than the dominant local culture simply 'bolted-on' by making chapattis and Divali lamps?

Do you know any stories, songs or nursery rhymes from cultures other than the one you were brought up in? Talk to children about the stories they are told at home.

Where can you go to develop your own knowledge and understanding about these issues? The 'Respect for all' web pages provide guidance and ideas on how your school can value diversity and challenge racism through the curriculum. The content is designed to help pupils from all ethnic groups and linguistic, social and cultural backgrounds realize their potential. It includes an 'anti-racist' toolkit and information about how to ensure all aspects of the curriculum are inclusive of ethnic minority cultures. www.qca.org.uk/qca_6753.aspx.

Case study

This case study looks at the importance of analysing and using the RAISE data to inform target-setting and other initiatives. A school in the South East looked at their data and interpreted what it was indicating about trends in children's achievement over the past five years in terms of the ethnicity of the children.

The previous five years had seen a marked change in the ethnic minority population of the school and local area, particularly in terms of the increased number of Polish families that had moved into the area and Polish children that were now attending the school. The school had already made links with the local authority support services to make necessary provision for children for whom English was an additional language, but felt more needed to be done to build links with parents. Through contacting the local Children's Centre and 'borrowing' the time and expertise of their community outreach worker they were able to make contact with a small group

continued

continued

of parents who were keen to work with the school to build closer home/school links.

The school discovered that the families were very supportive of the school, but that the education system the parents had experienced in Poland was very different from the English system, in English terms Polish schooling is much more formal, so sometimes parents were at a loss as to know why their children were doing certain things and how best to support them at home. Parents also struggled to read the detailed guidance which often used unfamiliar 'technical' terms about supporting reading that was sent home to them and needed considerable persuasion that it was good for the children to talk in Polish at home and to be able to read in Polish.

Over time, as both sides began to understand each other better, the school and parents have been very proactive together in finding ways to make the school more inclusive of the Polish culture. The school has taken on a Polish mother as a teaching assistant who has proved invaluable in supporting both the families and children. Information is produced in English and Polish, the school has links with the local adult education service and can now provide direct support for parents that want to develop their own English skills. The Polish TA runs regular story-telling sessions where Polish parents can come and tell stories in Polish as she translates them into English, which has been very successful in building links between communities.

In our busy day-to-day lives we can sometimes overlook why it is important to consider the experiences of marginalized groups of people. This section explores the experience of a particular ethic group as an example of why settings and schools need to ensure they are considering all aspects of Britain's ethnically diverse population.

Gypsy travellers

Gypsy traveller peoples have been one of the most persecuted ethnic groups in history, there are few European countries that do not have incidents in their past where they have passed laws to try and systematically force the Gypsy community to conform to the values, attitudes and beliefs of the settled cultures that dominate Europe. The most recent and ruthless attempt to extinguish the European Gypsy community was as part of Nazi Germany's race extermination holocaust in the late 1930s and up to 1945. During this time Gypsies were used for medical experimentation at Dachau, Buchenwald and Sachsenhausen, including, in 1941, experiments with 'Zyklon B gas crystals, later used in the death camps, were tested – fatally – on 250 Gypsy children' (Channel 4, 2008). It is estimated that 23,000 German Gypsies were sent to Auschwitz and that 19,000 perished. Gypsies were also persecuted under Stalin's regime in the Soviet Union and under the pro-Nazi Ustasa regime in Croatia. The famous Nazi hunter Simon Wiesenthal believed that: 'the Gypsies had been murdered [in a proportion] similar to the Jews' (Channel 4, 2008).

Many settings and schools have done a considerable amount of work towards enabling children and families from ethnic minorities to achieve economic well-being. However, in many instances Gypsy traveller children and families are still ignored and marginalized. Gypsy traveller children and their families have been identified since 1985 (DfES, 2003b: 3) as being subject to racism, discrimination and negative stereotyping, and still remain one of the most marginalized groups in society (DfES, 2003b: 3). Settings and schools have had success in working with Gypsy traveller children and their families where considerable effort has been made by the settings and schools to go out to the families, including those on sites, enroll the children in school and work with families to sustain attendance and raise achievement.

Whereas individuals in settings and schools often feel very confident in approaching families from cultures other than their own, often, because of the very negative dominant discourses about Gypsies and travellers that are prevalent in society, settings and schools feel far less confident in this area, starting with knowing the correct names to use when talking about the subject. The DfES (2003b: 3) guidance identifies a number of different groups that are happy to be called by the generic term traveller. Although, in effect, the travelling community is made up of a number of groups all of whom 'have a long tradition of a travelling lifestyle, although their history and customs vary' (DfES, 2003b: 3). In this way the travelling community is comprised of: 'English and Welsh Gypsies, Irish and Scottish Travellers, Showmen (Fairground people) and Circus people, Bargees (occupational boat dwellers) and New Travellers' (ibid.). While for families from travelling communities from 'Eastern and Central Europe "Roma" is very much the universally preferred term and Fairground people prefer to be called "Showmen".

It is estimated that approximately 350,000 of the Gypsy traveller community live in settled housing, while others 'live on local authority, or privately owned caravan sites or are resident on their own plot of land' (ibid.). It is estimated that it is about 20 per cent of the Gypsy traveller population for whom living in housing is not seen as something they want and therefore spend their time travelling. However, because of the decline in authorized sites over recent years (BBC, 2005a), they are often driven to setting up unauthorized encampments (DfES, 2003b: 3).

While mobility is the distinguishing feature of the travelling community and is one that has a long and rich heritage, it is the factor that causes the most tension between travelling people and settled communities. To a greater extent problems occur where a local authority has no authorized site and the local population perceives the arrival of a Gypsy encampment as bringing with it noise, mess and anti-social behaviour problems. These perceptions have been encouraged by recent media reporting, including one tabloid newspaper that ran a 'war' on what it termed the: 'Gypsy free-for-all' in response to government moves to support local authorities in setting up new sites for travelling people (Dear, 2005). In fact, even the most cursory research will show that where local authorities do have sites, the travelling population lives very well alongside the local settled population.

Ministers are clear that the solution to the current problems of unauthorised camping has to be a balance between effective enforcement and more authorised site provision. Well managed authorised sites can provide a sustainable solution for all concerned by reducing tensions between Gypsies and Travellers and the settled community, and also the costs to local taxpayers. Providing an authorised site can significantly reduce the need for costly enforcement action. One local authority has seen its enforcement costs drop from £200,000 to £5,000 a year, since building a new site. (Communities and Local Government, 2007)

Activity

Very often there is little in settings or schools that reflects the culture of this group of children and families. If you need to find out more about Romany and Gypsy culture, the following website and its related links, will be very useful: www.bbc.co.uk/kent/romany_roots/

This is a particularly powerful site, as you are able to hear Gypsies tell their own stories. Including stories about persecution and what it is like to live in a society that has as its dominant discourse a notion that the correct lifestyle is a settled lifestyle and that any alternative to this is a deviant way of living.

You can also access similar information about Gypsy and traveller studies at: www.dcauk.com/research/travellers.html

Activity

Below is a checklist of those things that setting or schools where children from Gypsy traveller families thrive, have in place. As you read through the list, consider which of the given elements you have seen in practice.

- Gypsy traveller culture is evident and celebrated around the setting or school along with many other cultures.
- The local authority's learning materials about the traveller community are readily available to adults – as are contact numbers for the relevant local authority traveller support services.
- Information about the history of Gypsy and traveller families is available.
- Training is provided for adults, by the local authority traveller support service.
- The setting or school knows how to provide uniforms and transport for Gypsy traveller children to help them to attend school, where necessary.
- Where appropriate Gypsy and traveller children receive intensive input on 'literacy and numeracy, it is in an atmosphere of calm and welcome and motivation'.

Many of these examples of good practice can be applied to raising the achievement of all children from all minority ethnic groups (OfSTED, 2005d: 7).

Class

Exploring the concept of class is important since, the capacity for children to realize long-term well-being is shown to still be affected by the class into which they are born. 'Classes are ... socially closed groupings in which distinctive cultures emerge and come to influence attitudes, behaviors, or even preferences of class members' (Grusky, 2005: 19). The concept of class has considerable bearing on our explorations of groups, identity and group culture, since while we can align ourselves in our attitudes, beliefs and values to various groups depending on our gender or ethnicity, we can also do so on the basis of class. Class differs from other forms of cultural groupings as it links those belonging to that group along shared identities and experiences linked to shared levels of educational achievement, occupations and, often, income. As with any group, that which its members share in common often binds members into the group and can keep them in the group when they may wish to leave, or not let others, who may wish to join the group, do so. Traditionally, in Britain, most children and families are seen as belonging to the working class or the middle class. Simply put, these two classes are primarily seen as being divided by occupation. Those who are defined as working-class undertake manual, non-professional occupations, while those in the middle class are in professional graduate occupations. Prior to some of the welfare reforms of the twentieth century the concern with class division was that the class you were born into would have a positive or negative affect on many of your other life-chances, your education, health and overall well-being. The changes in British society since the beginning of the twentieth century, including those related to potential earning capacity, private house ownership and education have, to some extent, made the working-class/middle-class division less clear and divisive. However, increasingly, over the past 10 years research has shown that there has perhaps been less of a shift in interclass mobility in British society than had previously been thought.

The notion of class is helpful in discussing poverty and the achievement of economic well-being, since what it does is move away from the notion of poverty being linked to cultures defined by ethnicity and identifies families, across cultures that are linked by other factor they have in common. For example, levels of education, income or health. Class becomes a consideration in terms of poverty, achieving economic well-being and being free from discrimination where the 'class' that any one child or family may be seen as belonging to has as part of its experience an expectation of low educational achievement, limited job opportunities and resulting low income, social denigration and exclusion (Grusky, 2005: 16).

These are important considerations, particularly when we are thinking about engaging children and families with education – as there may be a family history or attitude that is anti-education. It may also be the case some classes, particularly those characterized by lack of education and low-skill levels are more vulnerable to changes in economic climates and therefore less resilient than families in other classes. Education is seen as one of the main factors that can move children and families out of poverty and a university education is often seen as having the potential to allow the movement from reliance on less secure non-professional occupations with limited earning potential, to gaining a more secure professional job with a better salary. However, it is also the case that for vulnerable families education can be a risk too, particularly higher education at university level, where loans are needed to pay university fees and living expenses while at university. There is also a concern that it is too risky to invest in education since it is not guaranteed that the current deprivation of not having that family member working while they are studying, will indeed result in a significant financial 'pay-off' at some indeterminate time in the future. Class has become a recent focus for issues to do with attainment and the long-term impact of education on enabling children and families to achieve economic well-being, as the analysis of achievement data show that of the groups that are not achieving, white working-class children are among them – particularly white working-class boys (Bird and Fowler, 2004: 53).

Early intervention – education and extended schools

It has been increasingly recognized that the earlier support, be that health, education or other forms of support, is available to children and families (Barnett, 1998: 3: Van der Hoeven, 2003: 109) the greater the positive benefit the children and families will derive from it and the greater the likelihood of achieving the five ECM outcomes. Much has been done through the setting up of Children's Centres – often cited in this book as examples of good practice settings and schools can draw on to develop their own practice, in terms of exploring the support and early childcare that is available. In turn, the Children's Centres now in operation across England and with the full number being onstream for 2010 have built on the successes of the Head Start programmes in North America (Barnett, 1998) and the subsequent Sure Start programmes in England.

Research from Head Start and Sure Start has shown that where children have access to early support, children from families previously vulnerable to the risks discussed throughout this book have entered the formal education system better equipped to achieve (Barnett, 1998: 4). Other research (Rakodi, 2002) has shown that there is a link between good early experience of education and subsequent increased earnings. 'In addition, as education becomes more widely accessible, low-income people are better able to seek out economic opportunities, so there are positive effects on their well-being from both increased incomes and reduced fertility (Rakodi, 2002: 30).

Family support and resilience

Current child protection practice, and child development theory, recognizes that the best place for a child to be is with its family. However, it is also recognized that, for many reasons, many families may need varying levels of support for a short- to medium-term length of time, and others require more protracted support, to enable things to go well. Therefore, rather than removing children, which is a 'last resort', family support seeks to ensure the development and safety of children in their own family and to promote conditions in the family, school and neighbourhood conducive to such safety and development (Canavan, 2000: 14). Part of enabling a child to remain with their own family may be in supporting the whole family by preventing the breakdown of relationships within the family to the point where the children wish to leave for their own safety and welfare, or where other responsible adults feel this is necessary for the child[ren] (Canavan, 2000: 14). One way of supporting families is by connecting the child and family members to relevant support and resources and promoting morale and competence in parents (Canavan, 2000: 14).

Many families do have informal support networks through friends and their own extended families. Other families, for many reasons, may need a more planned approach involving the support of people with skills and experience in providing appropriate support, often these are professionals or para-professionals in, for instance, the health, social service or education systems (Canavan, 2000: 15). Such support may seek to strengthen the social supports and coping capacities of children and adults in the context of their families and neighbourhood (Canavan, 2000: 15). This could be through encouraging the family to become involved in support projects being offered locally. Support of this sort is precisely what Children's Centres are there to offer and many educational settings are building on the work undertaken by Children's Centres to continue to provide this support for children and families, through the Early Years and primary school phase. As we have seen in previous chapters, family support is central to the well-being of the child since family relationships are crucial to the well-being of everyone. Therefore, in seeking to support children and families in challenging circumstances, the concern is not to look only at what is 'wrong' with the family, that is, what it is about the family that does not fit the 'ideal', and blame that for the problems, but also to work with what the family does have that will enable it to overcome the current problems.

In Chapter 2 and 3 we briefly explored Bowlby's theory of the importance of children needing to form strong, secure attachments with significant adults in order to help them thrive, particularly in terms of their emotional well-being and in developing high levels of self-confidence. Not only do such attachments provide stability for a child, but they also teach them about trust in relationships and that the child themselves is of worth and is loved. In this way, successful support for vulnerable children is about ensuring they are safeguarded, but it is also 'about supporting children's social, psychological and educational development. It is about supporting their belonging to family, school and neighbourhood' (Canavan, 2000: 13).

What is family support?

Families that have severe problems may be ones where they are having to constantly change their address:

- leading to children experiencing disrupted education through frequent changes of school and possibly resulting in poor attendance;
- disrupted access to health services leading to crisis intervention rather than prevention;
- which will affect children's ability to make lasting friendships or get involved in regular activities;
- living in wholly unsuitable accommodation, with an increased likelihood of being exposed to risk;
- involvement in anti-social behaviour, often escalating into crime; and
- an increased risk of children being looked after within the statutory care system (Respect Family Intervention Projects, 2008).

For example, adults who were not parented appropriately themselves may simply not know how to parent their own children, and greatly benefit from support that can be offered in the initial stages of their children's lives. There are examples of very good practice in Children's Centres and other educational settings that provide extended/multi-agency services for children and their families, to help support the realization of this last ECM outcome – some of this is explored in Chapter 6. Besides the good practice being established in Children's Centres, there is also evidence that services offered by extended schools can break generational cycles of family behaviour that have not allowed families and children to achieve economic well-being.

The Protective Family Support Project

The government, through their Respect initiative fully support local authorities in using the protective family support approach to working with vulnerable families. Such approaches provide a range of support for the family, either for the family as a whole or including specific support for individual members of the family.

Such projects have found that children and families are vulnerable where family members have: poor anger control, may be misusing alcohol and drugs, lack parenting skills, cannot establish routines, may have unstable relationships, have low self-esteem, be isolated, have learning disabilities, health related issues, poor hygiene and nutrition, mental health problems, or be exhibiting traumatized behaviour, subject to social exclusion or offending/criminal behaviour and negative attitudes. They may have been reported by the wider community for anti-social behaviour, the most common forms occuring because of neighbour disputes, perhaps because of the behaviour of the children or poor upkeep of property.   *continued*

continued

The support workers and the family, or individual family members, as appropriate will work with the family to identified family strengths, for example: willingness to co-operate and make appropriate use of support/advice, willingness to take on board concerns/issues raised by professionals, as well as others. They will then focus on agreed key issues, for example: parenting, appropriate behaviour and language within the community and appropriate sanctions for managing behaviour.

Family members will then be given support in how to address the identified issues, for example, where a parent needs support on appropriate use of language at home, school and in the community, it may be that they need to be taught what language is regarded as 'good' and 'bad' and taught alternative ways of talking to their children and neighbours. They may need help in understanding how they seem to be presenting themselves to others and how to give and receive respect. For most very young and young children, to a greater extent their issues are related to the way they are being parented and, therefore, they will benefit from support being given to the parent(s), although some children will need a specific plan of support for themselves.

For older, teenaged children, for example, very specific support may be needed in the form of alcohol awareness sessions to cover the effects of alcohol, alcohol misuse and consequences for self, family and community, use of language. They may need encouragement to develop activities and interests, make appropriate friendships and be directly involved in planning for the future, identifying skills and strengths, and potential training opportunities.

Support will be undertaken by a range of people with appropriate skills and experiences, and may include: senior project workers, a key worker, antisocial behaviour workers, social workers, police (usually the police community support officers), workers from Job Centre Plus, youth resource workers and an education support worker.

These schemes are successful because they see that families that are vulnerable often have to deal with a range of issues and need support on a range of fronts. It is almost always the case that families needing this form of support are all on low incomes and many are headed by a lone parent.

Nearly all families who have been involved in these schemes are very encouraged by the project staff, who they see as supportive and understanding. Adults appreciated their access to better housing and to facilities and activities for their children, and most could see how they had developed personally and the improvement in family relationships. The children, too, welcomed improvements in their living conditions and responded well to a more routinized and 'organized' family, although some parents have found it hard to begin to take on all the responsibilities of maintaining the structures set up, as the support is withdrawn. (*Evaluation of the Dundee Families Project*, 2008: v–ix; Respect Family Intervention Projects, 2008).

It is the government's aim that by 2010 the provision that is currently being developed in Children's Centres should continue for children and families through all phases of education in schools, through them becoming Extended Schools, which will provide:

- access to childcare outside the school day;
- swift and easy referral to services families may need, for example health services;
- use of the setting's or school's facilities by the community;
- a varied menu of activities and parenting support. (OfSTED, 2006a: 2)

Through this provision it is intended that children will be provided with 'the opportunity to keep fit and healthy, to acquire new skills, to build on what they learn during the school day or simply to have fun and relax' (ibid.). With regard to extended schools, OfSTED has identified good practice as occurring where:

- cross-agency services have worked together to identify need and put services in place;
- settings and schools were effectively meeting all aspects of the ECM agenda, 'increasing their awareness of healthy eating and the importance of taking regular exercise as well as enjoying a range of activities';
- the extended services being offered benefited the wider communities in terms of the 'good quality services they received, such as on-site access to a range of professionals and health advice';
- settings and schools 'worked hard to take into account the differing needs and abilities within the community when organising provision';
- settings and schools liaised appropriately with local groups and agencies to ensure a coordinated approach to provision and responded to the outcomes of consultations;
- settings and schools developed their services alongside their communities to ensure needs were being met (OfSTED, 2006a: 2).

One of the most important points to come out of this research is that where extended services are working well, they have considerable positive impact on the confidence, self-esteem and achievement of all the adults and children using them (OfSTED, 2006a: 2). Consulting about, developing and planning the services also provided considerable opportunity for school councils to be involved in the process, thus increasing children's participation in the wider community and ensuring they had a platform where their voice was heard (OfSTED, 2006a: 5). 'Study support sessions provided the opportunity for pupils to work in a calm, secure environment where they could receive one-to-one help from teachers, especially if they had particular difficulties or if they were more able' (OfSTED, 2006a: 5).

Further benefits of successful extended services were identified as being:

- improvement in children's attendance and punctuality;

- in some instances the numbers of children on roll increased, due to the range of services on offer – including childcare;
- activities at breakfast clubs, which included conversation with adults and literacy work, enhanced children's language development and developed children's interest in reading (OfSTED, 2006a:6).

Time and again, where research into how to enable families to achieve economic well-being has been undertaken, there has been undeniable evidence to support the positive contribution that extended services have had on achieving this ECM outcome.

It seems that where settings and schools have sought to develop these services and have done so in consultation with the people that use them, both children and adults, the whole community has been stronger and better able to achieve economic well-being as a result. Adults comment that that they have increased self-confidence, that they feel more welcomed by the setting or school and that the knock-on affect from this is that they are more likely to seek advice and support from the setting or school over other issues. 'Services which had been used by the most vulnerable parents were reported to have transformed the lives of some parents and had positive effects on their children' (OfSTED, 2008a: 7).

Further reading

Department for Children, Schools and Families (DCFS) (2007e) *Extended Schools: Building on Experience*. London: HM Government.

Training and Development Agency (TDA) (2007) *Extended Services Toolkit for Governors*. London: Training and Development Agency.

Stobbs, P. (2008) *Extending Inclusion: Access for Disabled Children and Young People to Extended Schools and Children's Centres: A Development Manual*. London: DCSF/Council for Disabled Children.

Useful websites

The Index of Deprivation can be accessed at: www.communities.gov.uk/communities/

Information on valuing diversity and ethnicity through the curriculum can be found at: www.qca.org.uk/qca_6753.aspx

Information about Gypsy traveller peoples: www.bbc.co.uk/kent/romany_roots/ and www.dcauk.com/research/travellers.html

Conclusion

The intention of this book has been to help those who work with children, or intend to work with children, particularly in an Early Years setting or school, to deliver the Every Child Matters agenda and help children and families achieve its five outcomes. It has about enabling the achievement of well-being, and a central theme the book has explored is how our own attitudes, beliefs and values can impact on the ways in which we approach our role in this process.

We live in a highly complex and diverse society and as professionals it is part of our responsibility to ensure we are not confusing what we think is the case, or even what we would like to be the case, with what really is the case. We have seen how, for example, we can come to accept societal constructions of what we might mean when we talk about what children are, what childhood should be like and what the perfect family should look like. We have seen how, if we only use the dominant discourses about these concepts to shape and guide our attitudes towards children and families, we can be failing in our professional duty to meet the needs of real children and families, and possibly be failing to provide for them what they are entitled to.

Although the Every Child Matters outcomes for well-being are expressed in five short bullet points, unpacking what those aims mean for Early Years settings and schools, in terms of actual and potential policy and practice, has been a challenging and complex process. For example, where we have considered the 'being healthy' outcome, we have explored the importance of mental health as well as physical health and the concept of the need for children to develop resilience, if they are to achieve well-being in this aspect of their lives. We have acknowledged that relationship and sex education may be challenging to consider with very young children, but that we are more likely to ensure well-being in this aspect if we tackle it sensitively and appropriately throughout the time children are in settings or schools, rather than simply 'bolt-on' sex education and human reproduction at the end of primary school.

Similarly, in safeguarding children, while we know our responsibilities and our policy procedures that must be adhered to in ensuring a child is protected, particularly if we believe a child is in danger of maltreatment or abuse – or is being, maltreated or abused. We have also explored how to help the child and family develop strategies to ensure they are, where possible, able to safeguard themselves.

Settings and schools have long been expert in enabling children to enjoy and achieve in terms of their learning, but with the Every Child Matters agenda we are also challenged to ensure that we are giving children more control over the learning process. Through ensuring their learning is personalized, where it can be, to their interests, children are likely to be more motivated to learn. Similarly, through working with the child using Assessment for Learning techniques, we can help them develop skills, knowledge and understanding about structuring and managing their own learning, enthusing them to become lifelong learners.

The book has, many times, returned to the importance of children's voice and parents' voice and listening to and working with those voices to realize well-being. Not only does the concept of voice enable children and families to 'make a positive contribution' that benefits the wider community, but it also gives them the skills and confidence to protect themselves against discrimination. Having experience of being part of decision-making processes also helps children to develop self-confidence and deal with life-challenges, at, for example, important transition points in their lives.

The final aspect of the Every Child Matters agenda we have explored is the outcome that seeks to enable children and families to 'achieve economic well-being'. In exploring this concept we examined how factors in wider society can act against groups and individuals to prevent them enjoying this aspect of well-being; factors such as poverty, race and class. However, we have also seen how, through examining our own attitudes, values and beliefs and ensuring we work with children and families, seeking to provide appropriate support, for example, though extended services, families, and therefore their children, can be better enabled to achieve economic well-being now and in the longer term.

In our work, we need to leave aside the headlines in the press and approach individual children and families with an open mind. While we can believe we know what, in a perfect world, is the best practice in enabling children and their families to meet the five Every Child Matters outcomes, we also know that families come in all shapes and sizes, and that all families, at some time, are likely to need support to help them overcome minor crises or more long-term issues. In our examining of what constitutes families we have explored, as a central concept of this book, that being successful in achieving well-being, both for individual children and their families, is more likely to occur where settings and schools are working with their families to achieve it. While at any one time Early Years practitioners, or teachers, or health workers, or others will be able to give the best help and advice about a given situation, activity or challenge, at other times the experts we need to be consulting are the parents and, most of the time, we will get most insight into how to achieve the Every Child Matters outcomes if we listen to the children themselves.

Glossary

AfL	Assessment for Learning
BBC	British Broadcasting Corporation
CAMHS	Children and Adolescent Mental Health Service
CPS	Crown Prosecution Service
CWDC	Children's Workforce Development Council
DCSF	Department for Children, Schools and Families
DfEE	Department for Education and Employment
DfES	Department for Education and Skills
DPW	Department for Work and Pensions
EYFS	Early Years Foundation Stage framework
ECM	Every Child Matters
EY	Early Years
FS	Foundation Stage (children aged 3–4)
HM	Her Majesty's
HMI	Her Majesty's Inspectorate
HMSO	Her Majesty's Stationery Office
KS1	Key Stage 1 (children aged 5–7)
KS2	Key Stage 2 (children aged 8–11)
KS3	Key Stage 3 (children aged 12–14)
NC	National Curriculum
NSPCC	National Society for the Prevention of Cruelty to Children
OfSTED	Office for Standards in Education
PSED	Personal, Social and Emotional Development
PSHE	Personal, Social and Health Education
QAA	Quality and Assurance Agency
QCA	Qualifications and Curriculum Authority
TSO	The Stationery Office
UNCPC	United Nation's Convention on the Rights of the Child
UNCHR	United Nation's Convention on Human Rights

Bibliography

Adams, M., Bell, L.A. and Griffin, P. (eds) (2007) *Teaching for Diversity and Social Justice.* 2nd edn New York and London: Routledge Taylor and Francis Group.

Alderson, P. (2000) *Young Children's Rights: Exploring Beliefs, Principles and Practice.* London: Jessica Kingsley.

Alfrey, C. (ed.) (2003) *Understanding Children's Learning.* London: David Fulton.

Barber, B. (2007) *Consumed: How Markets Corrupt Children, Infantilize Adults, and Swallow Citizens Whole.* London: Norton.

Barnet, W.S. (ed.) (1998) *Early Care and Education for Children in Poverty.* London: State University of New York Press.

Barrett, L.F. (ed.) (2002) *Wisdom in Feeling: Psychological Processes in Emotional Intelligence.* New York: Guilford Publications.

Bastiani, J. and White, S. (2003) *Involving Parents, Raising Achievement.* London: DfES.

BBC (1999) *The Fall of King Coal,* http://news.bbc.co.uk/1/hi/business/551544.stm (accessed 10 August 2008).

BBC (2005a) *Gypsy Coalition Calls for Reform,* http://news.bbc.co.uk/1/hi/uk/4517033.stm (accessed 11 August 2008).

BBC (2005b) *Cameron Seeking 'Social Justice',* http://news.bbc.co.uk/1/hi/uk_politics/4507404.stm (accessed 16 July 2008).

BBC (2006) *School Dinner Row Meeting Held,* http://news.bbc.co.uk/1/hi/england/south_yorkshire/5357136.stm (accessed 11 April 2008).

BBC (2008) *UK Society 'Demonising' Children,* http://news.bbc.co.uk/1/hi/uk/7443104.stm (accessed 13 August 2008).

Beat Bullying (2008) *BBMentoring – What's It All About,* www.bbclic.com/index.php?option=com_content&task=view&id=28&Itemid=41&Itemid=41 (accessed 8 August 2008).

Bentham, S. (2004) *A Teaching Assistant's Guide to Child Development and Psychology in the Classroom.* London: RoutledgeFalmer.

Berk, L. (2004) *Awakening Children's Minds: How Parents and Teachers Can Make a Difference.* New York: Oxford University Press.

Bird, S. and Fowler, J. (2004) *School Improvement: Making Data Work.* Birmingham: The Education Network.

Black, P. (2003) *Assessment for Learning: Putting it into Practice.* Maidenhead: McGraw-Hill Educational.

Black, P. and Williams, D. (2001) *Inside the Black Box,* http://ngfl.northumberland.gov.uk/keystage3ictstrategy/Assessment/blackbox.pdf (accessed 4 August 2008).

Bonnie, R.J. (ed.) (2003) *Reducing Underage Drinking: A Collective Responsibility.* Washington, DC: National Academies Press.

Boucher, D. (ed.) (1998) *Social Justice: From Hume to Walzer.* New York: Routledge.

Brannen, J. (2000) *Connecting Children: Core and Family Life in Later Childhood.* London: Routledge.

Bridgeman, A. (ed.) (1998) *New Findings on Poverty and Child Health and Nutrition: Summary of a Research Briefing.* Washington, DC: National Academies Press.

Buhler, C. (ed.) (1999) *The Child and His Family.* London: Routledge.

Cameron, J.D. (2002) *Rewards and Intrinsic Motivation: Resolving the Controversy.* Westport, CT: Greenwood.

Canavan, J.R. (2000) *Family Support: Direction from Diversity.* London: Jessica Kingsley.

Cannella, G.S. (2002) *Kidworld: Childhood Studies, Global Perspectives and Education.* New York: Peter Lang.

Care Services and Improvement Partnership (2008) *What is the Children and Adolescent Mental Health Service?* www.camhs.org.uk/ (accessed 12 August 2008).

Chambers, D. (2001) *Representing the Family.* London: Sage Publications.

Channel 4 (2008) *The Holocaust: Gypsies,* www.channel4.com/history/microsites/H/holocaust/victims2.html (accessed 10 August 2008).

Child and Adolescent Mental Health Service (CAMHS) (2008) *Improving the Mental Health and Psychological Well-being of Children and Young People. National CAMHS Review Interim Report.* CAMHS.

Children Act 2004 – Guidance, www.everychildmatters.gov.uk/strategy/guidance/ (accessed 10 June 2008).

Children's Workforce Development Council (CWDC) (2007) *Common Assessment Framework for Children and Young People: Managers' Guide: Integrated Working to Improve Outcomes for Children and Young People.* Leeds: Children's Workforce Development Council.

Combrinck-Graham, L. (ed.) (2006) *Children in Family Contexts: Perspectives on Treatment.* 2nd edn. New York: Guilford.

Communities and Local Government (2007) *Gypsy and Traveller Sites Grant Guidance 2008–2011.* London: Department for Communities and Local Government.

Communities and Local Government (2008) *Indices of Deprivation 2007,* www.communities. gov.uk/communities/neighbourhoodrenewal/deprivation/deprivation07/ (accessed 10 August 2008).

Corby, B. (2005) *Child Abuse* (3rd edn). Maidenhead: McGraw Hill Education.

Crown Prosecution Service (2008) *Sentencing Manual: Sexual Offences S.15,* www. cps.gov.uk/legal/section15/chapter_p_15_18.html (accessed 13 September 2008).

Daniel, B. and Wassell, S. (2002a) *Early Years: Assessing and Promoting Resilience in Vulnerable Children.* London: Jessica Kingsley.

Daniel, B. and Wassell, S. (2002b) *Adolescence: Assessing and Promoting Resilience in Vulnerable Children.* London: Jessica Kingsley.

Daniel, B. and Wassell, S. (2002c) *School Years: Assessing and Promoting Resilience in Vulnerable Children.* London: Jessica Kingsley.

Daniel, B. (2004) *Child Neglect: Practice Issues for Health and Social Care.* London: Jessica Kingsley.

Dear, P. (2005) *Gypsy Campaign Raises Ethics Issues,* http://news.bbc.co.uk/ 1/hi/uk/4337281.stm (accessed 11 August 2008).

De Botton, A. (2001) *The Consolations of Philosophy.* London: Penguin.

Department for Children, Schools and Families (DCSF) (2007a) *Sure Start Children's Centres Practice Guidance.* London: DCSF.

Department for Children, Schools and Families (DCSF) (2007b) *Guidance on the Duty to promote Community Cohesion.* London: DCSF.

Department for Children, Schools and Families (DCSF) (2007c) *The Consolidated 3rd and 4th Periodic Report to the UN Committee on the Rights of the Child.* London: HM Government.

Department for Children, Schools and Families (DCSF) (2007d) *The Children's Plan: Building Brighter Futures.* London: TSO.

Department for Children, Schools and Families (DCFS) (2007e) *Extended Schools: Building on Experience.* London: HM Government.

Department for Children, Schools and Families (DCSF) (2008a) *Personalised Learning,* www.standards.dfes.gov.uk/personalisedlearning/about/ (accessed 5 August 2008).

Department for Children, Schools and Families (DCSF) (2008b) *Every Child Matters Outcomes Framework,* publications.everychildmatters.gov.uk/eOrderingDownload/ DCSF-00331–2008.pdf (accessed 6 August 2008).

Department for Children, Schools and Families (DCSF) (2008c) *Working Together: Listening to the Voices of Children and Young People.* London DCSF.

Department for Work and Pensions (DWP) (2008) *Households Below Average Income: An Analysis of the Income Distribution 1994/95–2006/07.* London: DWP.

Department of Health (2005) *Safeguarding Children in Whom Illness Is Fabricated or Induced.* London: Department of Health.

Department for Education and Employment (DfEE) (2000) *Sex and Relationship Education Guidance.* London: DfEE.

Department for Education and Employment/Qualifications and Curriculum Authority (DFEE/QCA) (1999) *The National Curriculum Handbook for Primary School Teachers.* London: DFEE/QCA

Department for Education and Skills (DfES) (2003a) *Aiming High: Raising the Achievement of Ethnic Minority Pupils.* London: DfES

Department for Education and Skills (DfES) (2003b) *Aiming High: Raising the Achievement of Gypsy Traveller Pupils.* London: DfES.

Department for Education and Skills (DfES) (2003c) *Materials for Schools: Involving Parents, Raising Achievement.* London: DfES.

Department for Education and Skills (DfES) (2003d) *Sustainable development action plan for education and skills.* London: DfES.

Department for Education and Skills (DfES) (2004a) *Choice for parents, the best start for children: a ten year strategy for childcare.* London: HMSO.

Department for Education and Skills (DfES) (2004b) *Every Child Matters: Change for Children in Schools.* London: DfES.

Department for Education and Skills (DfES) (2004c) *Healthy Living Blueprint for Schools.* London: DfES.

Department for Education and Skills (DfES) (2004d) *Putting the world into world-class education: an international strategy for education, skills and children's services.* (DfES/1077/2004).

Department for Education and Skills (DfES) (2004e) *Working together: giving children and young people a say* (DfES/0134/2004).

Department for Education and Skills (DfES) (2005) *Developing the Global Dimension in the School Curriculum.* London: DfES.

Department for Education and Skills (DfES) (2006) *What to Do If You Are Worried a Child Is Being Abused.* London: DFES.

Department for Education and Skills (DfES) (2007a) *Statutory Framework for the Early Years Foundation Stage.* London: DfES.

Department for Education and Skills (DfES) (2007b) *Practice Guidance for the Early Years Foundation Stage.* London: DfES.

Department for Education and Skills (DfES) (2007c) *Every Parent Matters.* London: DfES.

Directgov (2008) *Children's Human Rights,* www.direct.gov.uk/en/Parents/ParentsRights/

DG_4003313 (accessed 14 August 2008).

Donaldson, M. (1984) *Children's Minds.* London: Flamingo

Drew, E. (1998) *Women, Work and the Family in Europe.* London: Routledge.

Dwivedi, K.N. (2004) *Promoting Emotional Well-being of Children and Adolescence and Preventing Their Mental Ill Health: A Handbook.* London: Jessica Kingsley.

Emotional Health and Well-being (2008) www.healthyschools.gov.uk/ (accessed 31 July 2008).

Empson, J. (2004) *Atypical Child Development in Context.* London: Palgrave Macmillan.

Evaluation of the Dundee Families Project (2008) www.scotland.gov.uk/Resource/Doc/158816/0043123.pdf (accessed 17 May 2008).

Every Child Matters (2008) *Under-18 Conception Statistics 1998–2006,* www.everychild-matters.gov.uk/resources-and-practice/IG00200/ (accessed 8 May 2008).

Ferguson, H. (2004) *Protecting Children in Time: Child Abuse, Child Protection, and the Consequences of Modernity.* London: Palgrave Macmillan.

Fitzgerald, H.E. (ed.) (2000) *Children of Addiction: Research, Health and Public Policy Issues.* New York: Garland Science.

Flanagan, C. (1999) *Early Socialisation: Sociability and Attachment.* London: Routledge.

Foley, P., Roche, J. and Tucker, S. (2001) *Children in Society.* London: Palgrave

Freiberg, H.J. (1999) *Perceiving, Behaving, Becoming: Lessons Learned.* Alexandria, VA: Association for Supervision and Curriculum Development.

Gaine, C. and George, R. (1999) *Gender, 'Race' and Class in Schooling.* London: Falmer Press.

Gilbert, N. (1997) *Combating Child Abuse: International Perspectives and Trends.* New York: Oxford University Press.

Gibson-Graham, J.K. (ed.) (2000) *Class and its Others.* Minneapolis, MN: University of Minnesota Press.

Glantz, M. (ed.) (1999) *Resilience and Development: Positive Life Adaptations.* New York: Kluwer Academic.

Graham, P. (2007) *Rawls.* Oxford: Oneworld Publications.

Grusky, D.B. (ed.) (2005) *Poverty and Inequality.* Stanford, CA: Stanford University Press.

Gubrium, J. (2005) *Couples, Kids and Family Life.* New York: Oxford University Press.

Haskins, R. (ed.) (2001) *Welfare Reforms and Beyond.* Brooking International Press.

Healthy Eating (2008) www.healthyschools.gov.uk/ (accessed 31 July 2008).

Henry, C.M. (ed.) (2004) *Race, Poverty and Domestic Policy.* New Haven, CT: Yale University Press.

Hinman, L. (1998) *Ethics: A Pluralist Approach to Moral Theory,* 2nd edn. Fort Worth, TX: Harcourt Brace.

Hinman, L. (2003) *Ethics: A Pluralist Approach to Moral Theory,* 3rd edn. London: Thomson/Wadsworth.

HM Government (2006) *Working Together to Safeguard Children: A Guide to Inter-agency Working to Safeguard and Promote the Welfare of Children.* London: TSO.

Hoffman, J.S. (2004) *Youth Violence, Resilience and Rehabilitation.* El Paso, TX: LFB Scholarly Publishing.

Institute of Medicine Staff (2004) *Children's Health, the Nation's Wealth: Assessing and Improving Child Health.* Washington, DC: National Academies Press.

Jackson, P. (2001) *Social Scientists for Social Justice: Making the Case Against Segregation.* New York: New York University Press.

John, M. (2003) *Children's Rights and Power in a Changing World.* London: Jessica Kingsley.

Johnson, S.M. (ed.) (2003) *Attachment Processes in Couple and Family Therapy.* New York: Guilford.

Kimmel, J. (ed.) (2002) *Economics of Work and Family.* Kalamazoo, MI: W.E. Upjohn Institute for Employment Research.

Klein, R. (2003) *We Want Our Say.* Stoke-on-Trent: Trentham.

Knight, J. (2005) *The Changing Face of Poverty* http://news.bbc.co.uk/1/hi/business/4070112.stm (accessed 10 August 2008).

Knowles, G. (ed.) (2006) *Supporting Inclusive Practice.* London: David Fulton.

Lareau, A. (2003) *Unequal Childhood: The Importance of Social Class in Family Life.* Berkeley, CA: University of California Press.

Levine, J. (2002) *Harmful to Minors: The Perils of Protecting Children from Sex.* Minneapolis, MN: University of Minnesota Press.

Luke, C. (1989) *Pedagogy, Printing and Protestantism: The Discourse on Childhood.* New York: State University of New York Press

Lund, B. (2002) *Understanding State Welfare: Social Justice or Social Exclusion?* London: Sage Publications.

Lynn, A.B. (2001) *Emotional Intelligence Activity Book: 50 Activities for Promoting EQ at Work.* New York: AMACON.

March, J. (ed.) (2004) *Anxiety Disorders in Children and Adolescents,* 2nd edn. New York: Guilford.

Matheson, D. (2005) *Media Discourses.* Maidenhead: McGraw-Hill Education.

Michel, D. (2003) *When Dieting Becomes Dangerous: A Guide to Understanding and Treating Anorexia and Bulimia.* New Haven, CT: Yale University Press.

Miller, A. (2003) *Teachers, Parents and Classroom Behaviour: A Psychosocial Approach.* Maidenhead: McGraw-Hill Education.

Mills, J. (1999) *Childhood Studies: A Reader in Perspectives of Childhood.* London: Routledge Falmer.

Mills, S. (1997) *Discourse.* London: Routledge.

Morgan, D. (1996) *Family Connections.* Cambridge: Polity Press.

Muncie, J. (2004) *Youth and Crime,* 2nd edn. London: Sage Publications.

Naparstek, N. (2002) *Successful Educators: A Practical Guide for Understanding Children's Learning and Mental Health Issues.* Westport, CT: Greenwood.

Narey, M. (2007) 'Stop demonising children', *New Statesman,* www.newstatesman.com/life-and-society/2007/04/demonising-children-poverty (accessed 9 June 2008).

National Curriculum Online – Citizenship (2008) curriculum.qca.org.uk/key-stages-1-and-2/subjects/citizenship/keystage1/index.aspx?return=http%3A//curriculum.qca.org.uk/key-stages-1-and-2/subjects/index.aspx (accessed 10 June 2008).

National Healthy Schools Programme (NHSP) (2008) *In Brief.* London: NHSP.

National Society for the Prevention of Cruelty to Children (NSPCC) (2005) *Protecting Children from Sexual Abuse a Guide for Parents and Carers.* London: NSPCC Publications.

National Society for the Prevention of Cruelty to Children (NSPCC) (2008a) *Children's Rights,* www.nspcc.org.uk/whatwedo/mediacentre/mediabriefings/policy/children's_rights_media_briefing_wda49328.html (accessed 13 August 2008).

National Society for the Prevention of Cruelty to Children (NSPCC) (2008b) *Sexual Abuse,* www.nspcc.org.uk/helpandadvice/whatchildabuse/sexualabuse/sexualabuse_wda3670.html?gclid=CMPLmvmr-ZQCFQVxFQodMCClrQ#bookmark1 (accessed 6 August 2008).

Office for Standards in Education (OfSTED) (2002) *Sex and Relationships.* HMI.

Office for Standards in Education (OfSTED) (2003) *Yes He Can: Schools Where Boys Write Well.* London: HMI

Office for Standards in Education (OfSTED) (2004) *Transition from the Reception Year to Year 1.* HMI.

Office for Standards in Education (OfSTED) (2005a) *Drug Education in Schools.* HMI.

Office for Standards in Education (OfSTED) (2005b) *English 2000–05.* HMI/OfSTED.

Office for Standards in Education (OfSTED) (2005c) *Informing Practice in English.* HMI/OfSTED.

Office for Standards in Education (OfSTED) (2005d) *Race Equality in Education: Good*

Practice in Schools and Local Education Authorities. HMI.

Office for Standards in Education (OfSTED) (2005e) *Primary National Strategy: An Evaluation of its Impact in Primary Schools.* HMI.

Office for Standards in Education (OfSTED) (2006a) *Extended Services in Schools and Children's Centres.* HMI.

Office for Standards in Education (OfSTED) (2006b) *School Inspectors' Letters to Pupil: Lessons Learned and Ways Forward.* HMI.

Office for Standards in Education (OfSTED) (2007a) *Early Years Getting on Well; Enjoying and Achieving and Contributing.* HMI.

Office for Standards in Education (OfSTED) (2007b) *The Foundation Stage; a Survey of 144 settings.* HMI.

Office for Standards in Education (OfSTED) (2008a) *Children on Bullying: A Report by the Children's Rights Director for England.* HMI.

Office for Standards in Education (OfSTED) (2008b) *How Well Are They Doing? The Impact of Children's Centres and Extended Schools.* HMI.

Office for Standards in Education (OfSTED) (2008c) *Every Child Matters Framework for the Inspection of Schools in England from September 2005.* HMI.

Personal, Social and Health Education (2008) www.healthyschools.gov.uk/ (accessed 31 July 2008).

Peters, M., Seeds, K., Goldstein, A. and Coleman, N. (2008) *Parental Involvement in Children's Education 2007.* London: BMRB International/DCSF.

Physical Activity (2008) www.healthyschools.gov.uk/ (accessed 31 July 2008).

Plummer, D. (2005) *Helping Adolescents and Adults to Build Self-esteem.* London: Jessica Kingsley.

Qualifications and Curriculum Authority (QCA) (2008) *The 10 Principles: Assessment for Learning,* www.qca.org.uk/qca_4336.aspx (accessed 5 August 2008).

Rakodi, C. (ed.) (2002) *Urban Livelihoods: A People-Centred Approach to Reducing Poverty.* London: Earthscan Publications.

Randall, C. (1998) *Parental Right that Smacks of a Bygone Age,* www.corpun.com/ukdm9809.htm (accessed 6 August 2008).

Rawles, S. (2005) 'Where fathers figure', *Guardian,* 10 August, www.guardian.co.uk/society/2005/aug/10/childrensservices.guardiansocietysupplement (accessed 20 October 2008).

Respect Family Intervention Projects (2008) www.respect.gov.uk/uploadedFiles/Members_site/Documents_and_images/Supportive_interventions/FIP_Respect_Projects_0026.pdf (accessed 17 May 2008).

Ringold, D. (2004) *Roma in an Expanding Europe: Breaking the Poverty Cycle.* Washington, DC: World Bank Publications.

Robinson, K. (2005) *Diversity and Difference in Early Childhood Education: Issues for Theory and Practice.* Maidenhead: McGraw Hill.

Rose, E. (1999) *Mother's Job: The History of Day Care 1890–1960.* New York: Oxford University Press.

Rowan, E.L. (2006) *Understanding Child Sexual Abuse.* Jackson, MS: University Press of Mississippi.

Sanderson, C. (2004) *Seduction of Children: Empowering Parents and Teachers to Protect Children from Sexual Abuse.* London: Jessica Kingsley.

School Councils UK (2008a) Activity Guide 01, *Involving School Councils in OfSTED Inspections,* www.schoolcouncils.org/scuk_content/training_and_resources/Resources/Downloadable%20resources%20and%20tools/Activity%20Guides/scuk_tr (accessed 9 August 2008).

School Councils UK (2008b) Activity Guide 02, *Getting Involved in the Wider Community,* www.schoolcouncils.org/scuk_content/training_and_resources/Resources/Download

able%20resources%20and%20tools/Activity%20Guides/scuk_tr (accessed 9 August 2008).

School Councils UK (2008c) Activity Guide 03, *Getting your point across to adults in school,* www.schoolcouncils.org/scuk_content/training_and_resources/Resources/Download able%20resources%20and%20tools/Activity%20Guides/scuk_tr (accessed 9 August 2008).

Social Policy in the UK (2008) www2.rgu.ac.uk/publicpolicy/introduction/uk.htm (accessed 16 July 2008).

Stobbs, P. (2008) *Extending Inclusion Access for Disabled Children and Young People to Extended Schools and Children's Centres: A Development Manual.* London: DCSF/Council for Disabled Children.

Stokes, P. (2006) *Mrs Chips Takes Orders for the School Dinners Run,* www.telegraph.co.uk/news/main.jhtml?xml=/news/2006/09/16/nmeals16.xml (accessed 11 April 2008).

Sure Start (2005) *Birth to Three Matters: An Introduction to the Framework.* London: Sure Start.

The Liberty Guide to Human Rights (2008) *The Rights of Children and Young People: Introduction,* www.yourrights.org.uk/your-rights/chapters/the-rights-of-children-and-young-people/introduction/introduction.shtml (accessed 10 June 2008).

Thomas, N. (2000) *Children, Family and the State: Decision Making and Child Participation.* New York: St. Martin's Press.

Thompson, K. (1998) *Moral Panics.* London: Routledge.

Training and Development Agency (TDA) (2007) *Extended Services Toolkit for Governors.* London: Training and Development Agency.

UK Society 'Demonising' Children (2008) www.news.bbc.co.uk/1/hi/uk/7443104.stm (accessed 9 June 2008).

United Nations Conventions on the Rights of the Child (2008) www. everychildmatters. gov.uk/strategy/uncrc/ (accessed 10 June 2008).

Van der Hoeven, R. (ed.) (2003) *Perspectives on Growth and Poverty.* Tokyo: United Nations University Press.

Walkowitz, D.J. (1999) *Working with Class: Social Workers and the Politics of Middle-Class Identity.* Chapel Hill, NC: University of North Carolina Press.

Walsh, F. (2006) *Strengthening Family Resilience.* New York: Guilford.

Warsh, C.K. (ed.) (2005) *Children's Health: International Historic Perspectives.* Waterloo, ON: Wilfrid Laurier University Press.

Weiss, T.G. (2005) *UN Voices: the Struggle for Development and Social Justice.* Bloomington, IN: Indiana University Press.

Wissenberg, M.L.J. (1999) *Imperfection and Impartiality: An Outline of a Liberal Theory of Social Justice.* New Providence, NJ: BPR.

Womack, S. (2006) 'Punishing children by smacking wins widespread adult approval', www.telegraph.co.uk/news/1529321/Punishing-children-by-smacking-wins-widespread-adult-approval.html (accessed 6 August 2008).

Wyness, M. (1999) *Contesting Childhood.* London: Falmer Press.

Wyse, D. and Hawtin, A. (2000) *Children a Multi-professional Perspective.* London: Arnold.

Index